MS Works

An Active-Learning Approach

David Weale

David Weale has worked as an administrator at Bath University, as an accountant in professional practice, and is at present a lecturer in business computing at Yeovil College in Somerset.

DP Publications Ltd
Aldine Place
London W12 8AW
1992

Dedication

This book is dedicated to my wife, Annette who accepted sharing her piano room with the computer with good grace, and to my daughter, Rebecca who proof-checked the final version.

ISBN 1 873981 30 9

The text for this book was produced using MS Works

Printed in Great Britain by
The Guernsey Press Company Ltd
Braye Road
Vale
Guernsey
Channel Islands

CONTENTS

Preface

    1. Who should use this book 1

    2. The nature of the book 1

    3. The scope of the book 1

    4. The layout of the book 2

    5. How the book is organised 2

    6. Making effective use of the book 3

    7. After satisfactorily finishing the book 3

Loading Works 4

Works on-line help 5

How to use a mouse with Works 5

The Works tutorial 6

Sorting out problems 7

Keyboard characters 8

Word processing 9

Session 1 Getting started

    1. Objectives 10

    2. Opening a new file 11

    3. Entering text 12

    4. Saving on to disk 13

    5. Inserting text 14

    6. Deleting text 15

Session 2 Formatting
1. Objectives 17
2. Loading an existing document 17
3. Getting a graphics screen.........................18
4. Formatting text (bold, italics, underlining) 19
5. Removing character formatting....................20
6. Inserting a title 21
7. Centring text 21
8. Justifying text 21
9. Removing paragraph formatting 22
10. Double-spacing 22
11. Exercises...23
12. Hanging indents...................................24

Session 3 Tabs and tables
1. Objectives 26
2. To begin...26
3. Setting tabs 26
4. Setting decimal tabs...............................28

Session 4 Layout
1. Objective..29
2. To begin...29
3. Margins..29
4. Print preview.......................................30
5. Headers and footers 31
6. Moving text 34
7. Copying text 34
8. Paragraph indents.................................35
9. Page breaks..36
10. Printing text 36

Session 5 Spelling and Searching
1. Objectives 38
2. To begin...38
3. Spellchecking 38
4. The thesaurus 40
5. Searching for words 41
6. Replace 42

Session 6 Borders and Fonts
1. Objectives 44
2. To begin..44
3. Borders 44
4. Fonts...46

Session 7 Consolidation
1. Objectives 48
2. Tasks 48

Spreadsheets and Charts 50

Session 8 Spreadsheets
1. Objectives 51
2. Loading the spreadsheet 51
3. Entering text 52
4. Entering numbers 53

Session 9 Formulae
1. Objectives 55
2. Entering formulae...55
3. Copying formulae 57
4. Recalculation..57
5. Print preview..58
6. Printing the spreadsheet...58

Session 10 Layout and Format
1. Objectives 59
2. Inserting rows and columns 59
3. Deleting rows and columns..61
4. Altering column width..62
5. Formatting cells..63

Session 11 Editing and sorting
1. Objectives 66
2. Blanking cells 66
3. Entering other formulae...67
4. Tidying up the worksheet 68
5. Editing a cell 68
6. Sorting cells into order..69
7. Multiplying and dividing..70

Charting

Session 12 Graphs and charts
1. Objectives 72
2. To begin 72
3. Drawing a bar chart 72
4. Adding titles to a chart 73
5. Displaying legends 74
6. Viewing the chart 74
7. Adding grid lines to a graph 75
8. Drawing a stacked bar chart 75
9. Altering the font of the title 75

Session 13 Graphs and formulae
1. Objectives 78
2. To begin 78
3. Drawing line graphs 78
4. Creating a pie chart 79
5. Adding text to a pie chart 79

Session 14 Consolidation
1. Objectives 81
2. Tasks 81

Databases
.... 85

Session 15 Databases
1. Objectives 86
2. How a database is organised 86
3. To begin creating a database file 87
4. Creating a file structure 87
5. To enter field names on to the form 88
6. Altering the design of the form 89
7. Entering data on to the form 89
8. Looking at the data another way 90
9. Returning to form view 91
10. Adding records to the datafile 91
11. Sorting the datafile into order 92

Session 16 Searching
    1. Objectives 95
    2. Sorting on more than one field 95
    3. Searching for specific data 96
    4. Using wildcards 97
    5. Entering more than one search condition 97
    6. Other types of search condition 97
    7. Printing the records 98

Session 17 Reports
    1. Objectives 99
    2. Reports 100
    3. Changing character styles 102
    4. Entering the date into the report 103
    5. Adding additional text to the report 103
    6. Printing the report 103

Using MS Works in an integrated way 104

Session 18 Integrating Word Processed and Spreadsheet files
    1. Objectives 105
    2. To start 105
    3. Copying figures from the spreadsheet 106
    4. Copying a chart from the spreadsheet 107
    5. Looking at how the chart will actually appear 107
    6. Altering the size of the chart 107

Session 19 Mailmerging
    1. Objectives 109
    2. To begin 109
    3. Creating a form letter 109

**Session 20 Final exercise - incorporating spreadsheets,
word processing and databases** 112

Appendices..115

Appendix 1 Suggestions on layout
    1. Character commands 116
    2. Paragraph commands 116
    3. Page commands 116
    4. Experiment......................................117
Appendix 2 Summary of commands
    1. File commands 118
    2. Word processing 119
    3. Spreadsheets 121
    4. Charting 122
    5. Databases.......................................122
    6. Copying 123
Appendix 3 File management..................124
Appendix 4 Configuring the system..........127

Preface

1. Who should use this book

This manual has been designed as a self-teaching book which readers can use at their own pace. The contents are self-explanatory and should not require any outside assistance.

The book was written for students and business persons who want to learn the program quickly and effectively.

2. The nature of the book

The manual was designed to take students through the elements of the program, without expecting any pre-knowledge of the program from them.

Unlike many of the expensive computer manuals and books on the market, this is **not** a rewrite of the original program manual, but a step by step guide, which deals with the commands in a simple and easily digested way and allows the reader to learn while actually using the program.

3. The scope of the book

The idea behind this book is for the reader to learn and practice the commands and techniques of the program, building from the very simple and basic level to the relatively sophisticated.

Obviously a book of this nature cannot cover every single aspect of the program, but experience has shown that having covered the material in this book, the reader will be able to master any other aspects of the program by reference to the program manual supplied with the MS-Works program.

4. The layout of the book

This book is laid out as a series of sessions, each session being self-contained and capable of being covered reasonably quickly. You should not need to spend more than an hour on any of the sessions (except for the later consolidation sections which may take longer.)

The book is divided into four main areas:

Word processing
Spreadsheets
Databases
Using MS Works in an integrated way

Each section contains several sessions with a consolidation session to check on the your understanding and to enable you to revise the most important elements.

There are also Appendices dealing with File Management, Layout of documents and a list of commands for your future reference.

5. How the book is organised

The book is organised so that as each type of activity is introduced, you begin immediately to create your own documents and files. These files are developed through the sessions and when you have become familiar with the use of word processing, spreadsheets, charting and databases, then you learn how to integrate them together, for example how to combine a chart with text in the form of a report.

The Appendices contain both reference material and notes on other topics such as how to layout your work effectively and how to carry out disk housekeeping tasks. I suggest you read the Appendices when you are consolidating your knowledge or when you have worked through the rest of the book.

6. Making effective use of the book

To make the best use of the book it is worthwhile following these simple guide-lines.

Make sure that you read each instruction carefully and follow them exactly (if you don't do this you may achieve unexpected results).

Make sure you have completed each session correctly *before* going on to the next. If problems arise in one session, go through it again until you are confident.

There is not a race to finish the book.

7. After satisfactorily finishing the book

When you have covered all the areas in the book, read the program manual supplied with MS-Works. You will be surprised how much of it has been covered and how easy the MS-Works manual is to understand (even if it seemed hard before you used this manual).

Loading Works

There are different ways in which you can load Works on your computer system. These assume that Works has been successfully installed onto your system. If it has not then you should follow the installation procedure you received with the program discs and manuals.

1. From the DOS prompt

If you do not have a menu program set up on your system then when you switch the system on, you get a screen similar to this:

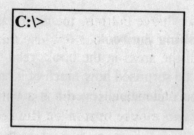

At this stage all that is necessary is for you to type **WORKS** followed by the **return** key. Works will load and you will be presented with the initial screen (see session 1).

If this results in an error message then try typing the following (at the C:\> prompt)

CD WORKS   followed by the **return** key
WORKS   followed by the **return** key

2. From a menu

If you have a menu program installed then it is even easier, just follow through the menu options until Works is loaded.

Works on-line help

WORKS includes **HELP** screens which can be called up either by pressing **F1** or by pulling down the **Help** menu (**ALT H**).

How to use a mouse with Works

The cursor can be moved around the screen and commands can be selected using the keyboard and/or **a mouse**.

Your mouse may have two or three buttons, the most used is the left hand one, some programs make use of the right button, but few use the middle one (if you actually have three.)

The manual lists the keyboard commands in the text but if you want to use a mouse then simply **click the left hand mouse button on the required command** and it will be carried out.

Almost every activity within WORKS (apart from entering text) can be carried out by using a mouse, for example to select a file **double-click** (quickly) the left mouse button on the filename and the file is loaded.

Using a mouse is much easier than using the keyboard (once you are used to using one) and it is worth persevering with its use even if it appears difficult at first.

The Works tutorial

The WORKS program includes a tutorial which first-time users of the program should go through before attempting to use the program itself. It provides a good introduction to the program and is especially helpful to newcomers to computing as it explains the various elements of WORKS.

The tutorial consists of six parts

works essentials
word-processing
spreadsheets and charts
databases and reports
using the tools together
communications

You can use the tutorial from within the program by pulling down the **Help** menu (**ALT H**) and pressing **W** (for **Works Tutorial**).

The tutorial explains the program and only allows you very limited practise in using the commands. It is an overview and should be treated as such. You can usefully spend anything from half an hour to several hours familiarising yourself with the program tutorial, depending upon your previous experience and aptitude.

I suggest you look at the tutorial in stages before using that part of the program, but please do the Works Essentials part of the tutorial before beginning the program.

Sorting out problems

If you do have problems either installing Works, getting it to load or to run successfully then there are various avenues open to you.

1.   Ask someone else who may know the answer e.g. your computer lecturer.

2.   Contact the supplier of the program or the Microsoft customer support department.

3.   Contact the firm who supplied the computer system itself.

4.   Read the manuals that came with the program.

Keyboard characters

Most of the keys on the keyboard are self explanatory, here are some of the less obvious ones

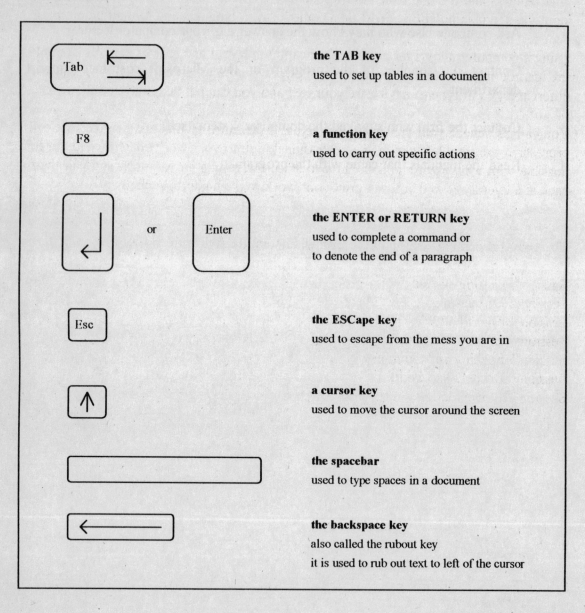

the TAB key
used to set up tables in a document

a function key
used to carry out specific actions

the ENTER or RETURN key
used to complete a command or
to denote the end of a paragraph

the ESCape key
used to escape from the mess you are in

a cursor key
used to move the cursor around the screen

the spacebar
used to type spaces in a document

the backspace key
also called the rubout key
it is used to rub out text to left of the cursor

Word Processing

The practical sessions begin with word processing, this is the most popular application of computers and the one which most people are familiar with. Word processing is the inputting and manipulation of text on a computer e.g. typing in and formatting a report.

Using a computer allows far more sophistication in layout and ease of use, for example text can be moved around the document, errors can be easily corrected, you can use different styles of type to emphasise your text and you can put boxes around the text.

You can also check your spelling and even use a thesaurus to find new words. A word processing program lets you give a professional look to your work which would not be possible with a typewriter. You can also store the results on to a disk and call them back at a later stage and you can print your work to the highest standards.

The word processing section of the manual contain the following sessions:

Session 1 Getting started
Session 2 Formatting
Session 3 Tabs and tables
Session 4 Layout
Session 5 Spelling and Searching
Session 6 Borders and Fonts
Session 7 Consolidation

SESSION 1

Getting started

---

1. Objectives

By the end of this session you will be able to:
Open a new file.
Enter and alter text.
Insert and delete text.
Save text onto the disc.

Suggestions

Work slowly to make sure you understand what you have done.
Read and carry out the instructions carefully.
Look at what has happened on the screen.

---

2. Opening a new file

After having loaded **Works**, the **File** menu will be displayed on screen (below).

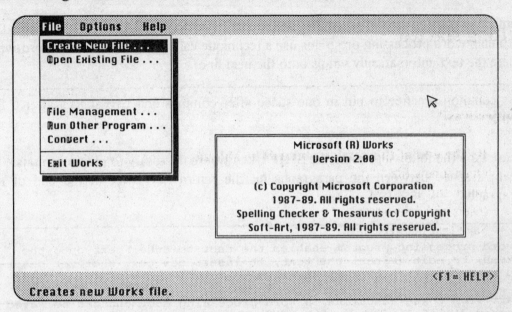

To select an option from a menu just type the highlighted character (in the name). In this case press the **N** key (for **Create New File**), at which point the screen will change to this:

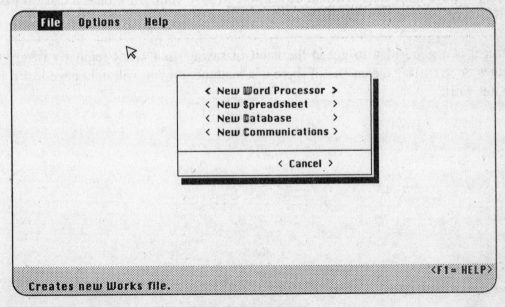

Then press the **W** key (for **New Word Processor**).

3. Entering text
Now you can begin to type text onto the screen.

Remember **only** to hit the return key at the end of each paragraph (**NOT** at the end of each line, word processing programs use a technique called wrap-around or word-wrap where the text automatically wraps onto the next line).

It is common practice to put in one space after commas and two spaces after a full stop.

Please type the following, using the **SHIFT** key where necessary to obtain capitals. To create a space between the paragraphs hit the return key twice at the end of the paragraph.

```
A word-processing program enables the user to enter text onto the
screen, to edit (alter) the text, to insert new text wherever desired
and to delete text that is unwanted.

Apart from these functions, a word-processing document can be saved
(recorded) onto a floppy or hard disc and recalled at a later date.
It can then be changed as necessary.
```

When you have done this, it would be sensible to save your work onto a disk so that if anything goes wrong, the original could be recalled.

In fact it is a good idea to get in the habit of saving your work regularly (every ten minutes or so). This means that if there is a malfunction you will only have lost a few minutes work.

4. Saving onto disk

To save your work use the keys **ALT F** again to pull down the **File** menu (remembering to hold the first key down while pressing the second key). You will see the following screen:

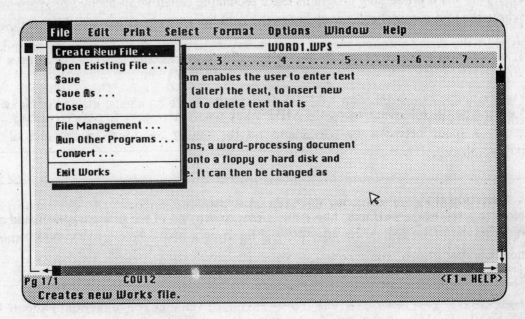

Press the **A** key (for **Save As**), this enables you to give the file a specific name. The screen will look like this:

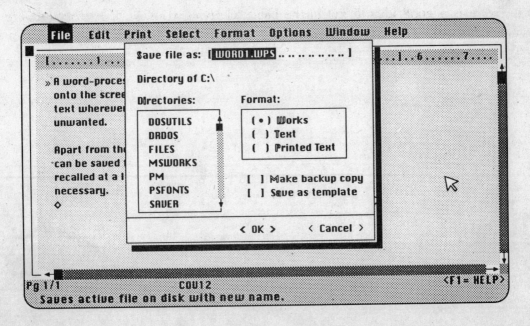

Type the name you wish to call the file (up to eight characters, but **NO** full stops or spaces), and press the **RETURN** (or **Enter**) key. The file is saved on disk.

Notes

Files are given a three letter extension automatically (as this is the standard extension used by the disk operating system commands), notice how the letters WPS are added to the name you call your file.

Once you have named the file, you can then use the **Save** command instead of **Save As** (this is quicker).

---

5. Inserting text

Now to insert some new text, move the cursor to the end of the first paragraph and add the following text straight on after the end (starting a new sentence). Do **NOT** start a new paragraph.

```
Additional features are the formatting of the text, characters can be
in bold, italic, they can be underlined and paragraphs can be
justified (this means having a straight right hand margin, as well as
the normal straight left hand margin).
```

At this point the screen should look like this:

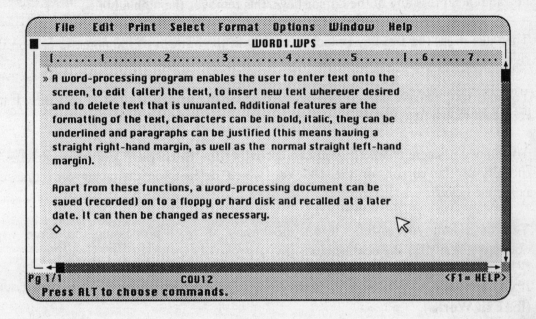

```
   File   Edit   Print   Select   Format   Options   Window   Help
■────────────────────────── WORD1.WPS ──────────────────────────
  [.......1.........2.........3.........4.........5......|.6.....7....
» A word-processing program enables the user to enter text onto the
  screen, to edit (alter) the text, to insert new text wherever desired
  and to delete text that is unwanted. Additional features are the
  formatting of the text, characters can be in bold, italic, they can be
  underlined and paragraphs can be justified (this means having a
  straight right-hand margin, as well as the  normal straight left-hand
  margin).

  Apart from these functions, a word-processing document can be
  saved (recorded) on to a floppy or hard disk and recalled at a later
  date. It can then be changed as necessary.
  ◇                                                    �

Pg 1/1                      COU12                              <F1 = HELP>
  Press ALT to choose commands.
```

6. Deleting text

Having inserted text into your document, you can now learn how to delete unwanted text.

In this case we have decided to take out the last nine words of the first paragraph, the words to be deleted are:

```
as well as the normal straight left hand margin
```

To do this move the cursor to the end of the paragraph (by using the cursor keys) and press the function key **F8** (this is called the extend key).

Then keep pressing the cursor key until all the required text is highlighted.

If using the mouse, click the left hand mouse button on the first character and **still holding down the mouse button** drag the mouse so that the highlighting covers all the necessary text, then let go of the mouse button.

If you highlight too much text, or generally mess up the highlighting, press the **ESC** key and then press any of the cursor keys, this removes the highlighting.

Then just press the **Del** key (which is usually at the bottom of the numeric pad on the right of the keyboard).

To finish off, remove the comma at the end of the sentence (if it is still there) and replace it with a full stop.

To remove a single character you can use either the **Backspace** key which deletes to the left of the cursor, or the **Del** key which deletes the character the cursor is positioned over.

You have now successfully learnt the basics of word-processing, so **Save** your document, ready for the next session.

If you are finishing now quit WORKS by selecting the **File menu** and then typing **X** (for **Exit Works)**.

If you are continuing turn to the next session.

SESSION 2

Formatting

---

1. Objectives
   At the end of this session you will be able to:
   Retrieve a file that has previously been saved on disk.
   Format text (bold, italic and underlining).
   Carry out paragraph formatting (justification and double line spacing).
   Create hanging indents.

---

2. Loading an existing document

After loading WORKS, load your document by typing **O** (for **Open Existing File**). The following screen will appear:

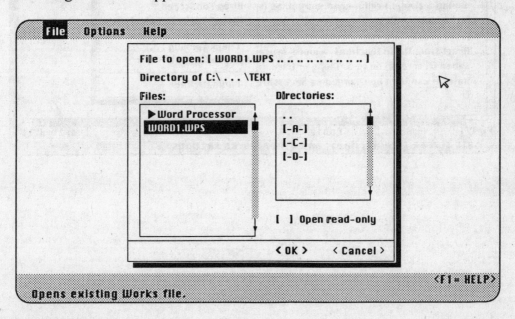

Then type **ALT F** (for **File**) and move the cursor onto your filename and hit **RETURN**. This will load your document onto the screen.

17

3. Getting a graphics screen
WORKS can be viewed in two modes, Text and Graphics.

At present you are probably in **text mode** (where the underlining, bold and italics are shown as colours).

Graphics mode shows underlining, bold and italics as they will print out, older text screens can't do this and used different shades or colours instead. It is far better to use graphics mode as you can see the effect of your formatting instructions.

Pull down the **Options** menu (**ALT O**), which looks like this:

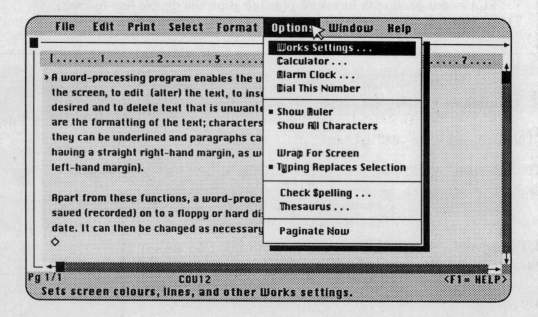

Select **Works Settings (W)**, and the following screen will appear:

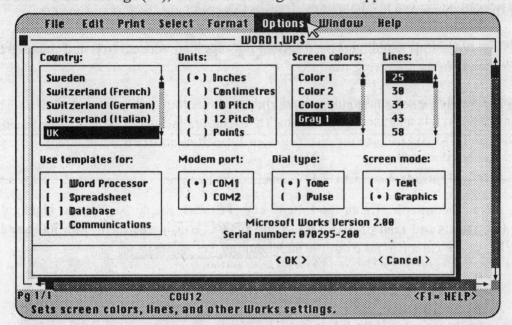

Then select **Alt G** (for **Graphics**) and press **Return**.

The screen will blank and then re-appear in the graphics mode. (For more details about the various options see appendix 4, **Configuring the System**).

4. Formatting text (bold, italic, underlining)
Now to format the text (formatting means making the text bold or italic etc.).

Move the cursor onto the first character of the first paragraph.

Press the **extend key (F8)** and then move the cursor across the first three words in that paragraph i.e.

```
A word-processing program
```

These three words are now highlighted. To change the type to bold hold the **CTRL** key and press the **B** key (or pull down the **Format** menu and select **Bold**). Move the cursor off the words to see the effect.

Now highlight those three words again and this time press **CTRL** and **U**. This has the effect of underlining the highlighted text (again you could use the **Format** menu).

These two operations could have been carried out together, without having to highlight the text twice, in the following way.

Move the cursor onto the first character of the words

saved (recorded)

in the second paragraph. Using the Extend key (**F8**) and the cursor keys to highlight these two words and then press **CTRL I** and **CTRL B** to make them both italic and bold. Move the cursor to take out the highlighting.

Your screen will be similar to this:

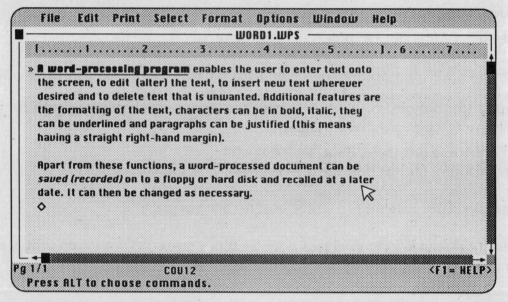

5. Removing character formatting
To remove character formatting highlight the text and then type **CTRL** and **space-bar** (holding the CTRL key down while pressing the space-bar).

To practise, highlight the first three words in the first paragraph and remove the formatting.

6. Inserting a title

The text on your screen needs a title. To do this, move the cursor to the top of the document (**CTRL HOME**) and press **RETURN**.

Move the cursor back to top of the text and type the following heading:

```
A simple introduction to computing
```

7. Centring text

Highlight the title and format it to bold, underline and italic.

Then centre it by using **CTRL C**.

8. Justifying text

Highlight all the text by pressing the extend key **F8** several times.

Then type **ALT T** (for **Format**), this pulls down the **Format** menu.

Type **J** (for **Justified**) and move the cursor (to remove the highlighting). All the text will have a straight right hand margin.

Note how the title has lost its centring, re-centre it.

At this point the text will look like this:

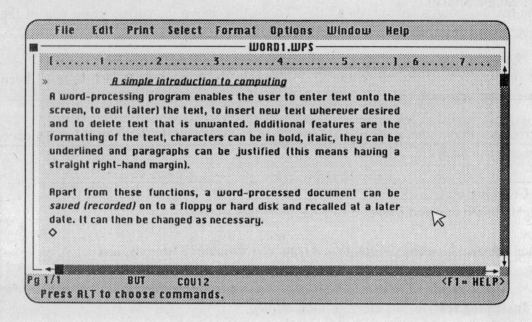

9. Removing paragraph formatting

Now move the cursor to anywhere within the first paragraph. Highlight this paragraph by pressing the extend key (four times).

Then type **ALT T** (for **Format**), this pulls down the **Format menu**. Type **N** (for **Normal Paragraph**), this removes all the paragraph formatting. Move the cursor to take out the highlighting.

Note how this has removed the justification.

10. Double-spacing

Now we will format the first paragraph on its own and leave the remainder of the text alone.

To do this highlight just the first paragraph again.

Then to give double space format, type **ALT T** and then **D** (for **Double Space**). Move the cursor to take out the highlighting and see the effect.

Now remove the double line spacing by highlighting the text, typing **ALT T** and then **S** (for **Single Space**).

11. Exercises

To practise, try to do the following, looking up the commands (which have all been covered) if you need to.

Remember that at this stage you are trying not to memorise the commands but get used to using the program.

---

i. Highlight all the text.

ii. Remove all the paragraph and character formatting from the text.

   You need to remove both the character formatting (bold etc.) and the paragraph (justification etc.) formatting.

   These were both covered earlier in this session.

iii. Highlight the words `floppy` or `hard disc` (in the second paragraph), and format them to italic and underlined.

iv. Format the words `word-processing document` (again in the second paragraph) to bold.

v. Format all the text to double line spacing, and justify all the text.

vi. Centre and underline the title.

vii. Save the text onto a disk.

---

12. Hanging indents

Another useful technique is that of using hanging indents to lay out paragraphs (especially if the paragraphs are to be numbered).

To do this move the cursor to the first character of the first paragraph. Then type the number 1.

Press the **TAB** key to move the text across the page (but leaving the number where it was).

Now type **CTRL H** (for **hanging indent**). This lines up the second, third (etc) lines with the first.

It is important to remember that CTRL H only works on the second and following lines, the first line always has to be tabbed across.

A hanging indent looks like this:

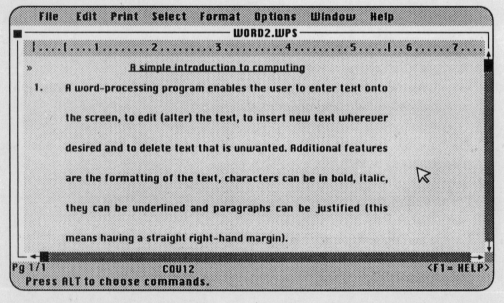

To remove hanging indents (if you have put in too many or have put one in the wrong paragraph, press **CTRL G**).

Number and indent the second paragraph in the same way as the first.

Save the file.

> The layout of the finished result should look similar to this:

<u>A simple introduction to computing</u>

1   A word-processing program enables the user to enter text onto the screen, to edit (alter) the text, to insert new text wherever desired and to delete text that is unwanted.   Additional features are the formatting of the text, characters can be in bold, italic, they can be underlined and paragraphs can be justified (this means having a straight right hand margin).

2   Apart from these functions, a **word-processing document** can be saved (recorded) onto a *<u>floppy or hard disc</u>* and recalled at a later date.   It can then be changed as necessary.

SESSION 3

Tabs and tables

---

1. Objectives
   At the end of this session you will be able to:
   Set tabs and create tables.

---

2. To begin
Create a **New Word Processor** file (see Session 1 if you cannot remember how to do this).

3. Setting tabs
A tab is a preset marker on the page which can be used for formatting purposes. Pressing the tab key sends the cursor to the next tab marker - either the tab you have set or the default tab markers (at half inch intervals on most programs).

To begin setting tabs, pull down the **Format** menu and select **T** (for **Tabs**).

Enter the number **2** in the **Position box**, enter **ALT L** (for **Left**), **ALT N** (for **None**) and then type **ALT I** (for **Insert**).

Look at the ruler at the top of the screen and you will see a **L** (for left tab) at the 2 inch position. The screen will look like this:

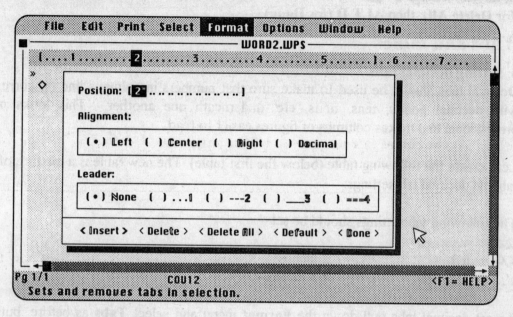

Now create another tab stop at the 4.5 inch position, by going through the same procedure as before. Overtype the original figure and set a left tab as shown above.

When all the tabs have been set type **ALT D** (for **Done**).

Enter the following table. Use the **Tab** key to move across the page. (Do the underlining after the table has been finished).

Complete each line before moving down to the next by **Return**ing. (When using tabs it is important to move down by using the **Return** key, otherwise the tab setting can be lost.)

Disk Size	Type	Capacity
3.5"	D/Density	720 Kbytes
3.5"	H/Density	1.44 Mbytes
5.25"	D/Density	360 Kbytes
5.25"	H/Density	1.2 Mbytes

H/Density = High density
D/Density = Double Density

After entering the table make sure that the cursor is below the original text, then clear all the tab settings by pulling down the **Format** menu and selecting **Tabs** and **ALT A** (for **Delete All**), then **ALT D** (for **Done**).

4. Setting decimal tabs

Decimal tabs should be used to make sure that numbers in columns line up correctly, with decimal points, tens, units, etc. underneath one another. This looks more professional and makes columns of figures easier to read.

Let's create the following table (below the first table). The new table is a mixture of left tab and decimal tab settings.

The following tab settings should be set:

left	2 inches
decimal	4.5 inches

To set decimal tabs pull down the **Format** menu and select **Tabs** as before, but this time after entering the position type **ALT E** (for **Decimal**) and **ALT N** (for **None**), then **ALT I** (for **Insert**).

After having finished setting the tabs, look at the ruler, you can see the **L** and **D** which stand for **Left** and **Decimal** tabs. Look at how the figures arrange themselves as you type them in.

```
Type of Program      Name                  Cost
Word-processing      Word v.5.5             267
                     Wordperfect v.5.1      267
                     Wordstar 2000+         247
Integrated           Works v.2              99
```

Save the file under a **different name** from your first file.

> If it is saved under the same name, the original file will be overwritten by the new one, thus destroying the original.

SESSION 4

Layout

---

1. Objectives

At the end of this session you will have covered the following:
Headers and Footers
Page Numbers
Print Preview
Changing Margins
Moving and copying text
Paragraph indents
Page breaks
Printing

---

2. To begin
Open the document you saved at the end of session 2.

3. Margins
For several reasons (layout, size of paper etc.) you may wish to alter the margins from those already set.

To do this type **ALT P** to pull down the **Print** menu and then **M** (for **Page Setup & Margins**).

A new screen will appear, all that is required is for you to fill in the relevant measurements and **Return** when finished. Use the **Tab** key to move between the boxes.

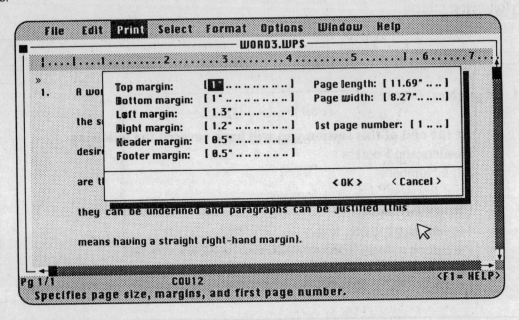

Change the left margin to 2 inches and the right margin to 3 inches.

It can be seen that when the margins are changed on the normal screen that the left margin does not appear to alter, whereas the right margin does.

This is deliberate so that as much text can be displayed on the screen at one time.

However when using **Print Preview** (described below) the layout is displayed properly.

4. Print preview
This enables you to see how the text will appear on the printed page and gives a good indication of spacing, headers and footers etc.

To do this:

Pull down the **Print** menu **ALT P** and type **V** for **Preview**. You should see the following screen

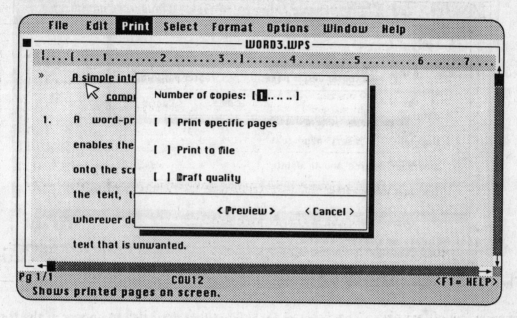

After having done this type **ALT P** (for **Preview**).

You can now see how your document will look like when printed, this is useful since it can now be altered if necessary without the time and expense of printing it out.

If there is more than one page move between the different pages of your document use **PgUp** and **PgDn** keys.

To get back to the normal screen press the **ESC** key.

5. Headers and footers
Headers and Footers are text which appear at the top or bottom of every page, for example the title of a chapter or page numbers.

To create these, pull down the **Print** menu by typing **ALT P**, then **H** (for **Headers and Footers**).

word processing

Type **ALT U** (for **Use header & footer paragraphs**), The screen will look like this:

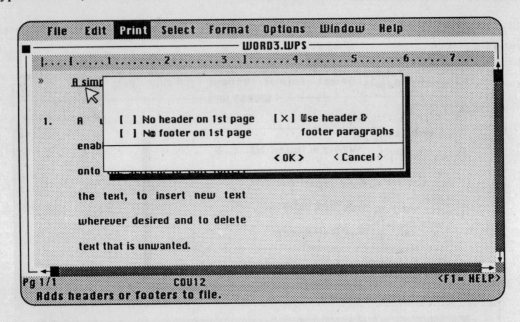

Then **Return**, and a **H** and **F** will appear at the top of the screen.

These stand for **Header** and **Footer** and whatever text you wish to appear at the top or bottom of each page should be typed on the appropriate line.

If you look at the **Footer** line, there may already be shown

Page - *page*

(if not then type the word **Page** and then hold the **CTRL** and **P** keys down)

This means that page numbers will automatically appear on each page.

At this point the screen should look like this:

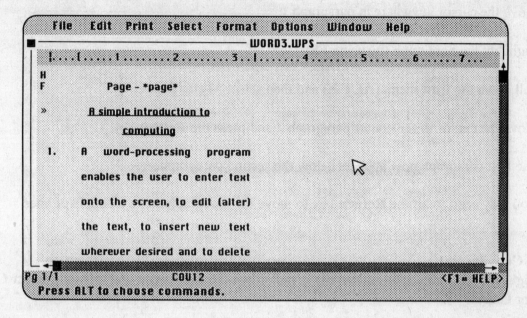

If you do not want the page numbers then highlight and delete the text.

Type your name on the **Header** line and format it into bold italics, and then centre it.

Now use the **Print Preview** command (described above) to see how this would look when printed out.

If this was successful, you can see the header (showing your name) and the footer (showing the page number).

Now change the margins back to the original measurements (left 1.3", right 1.2") and again use **Print Preview** to see the revised effect.

6. Moving text

Move the cursor anywhere in paragraph 1.

Highlight the paragraph (by using **F8**).

Pull down the **Edit** menu (**ALT E**) and then select **M** (for **Move**).

Move the cursor to the end of paragraph 2 and press the **Return** key.

The first paragraph now appears below the second paragraph.

You may need to hit the **Return** key to move the paragraph down a couple of lines.

7. Copying text

Highlight the paragraph (numbered) 2, pull down the **Edit** menu and this time select **C** (for **Copy**).

Move the cursor to the bottom of the text and press the **Return** key and **Return** again to move the paragraph down.

The paragraph has been copied, and thus appears twice, once at the top and once at the bottom.

To tidy up the text, remove the paragraph at the top of the page as it is superfluous (do this by highlighting it and pressing the **Del** key).

The text should now be in the same state as it began this session.

8. Paragraph indents

Highlight the first paragraph and then pull down the **Format** menu (**ALT T**) and select **A** (for **Indents & Spacing**). The following screen will appear:

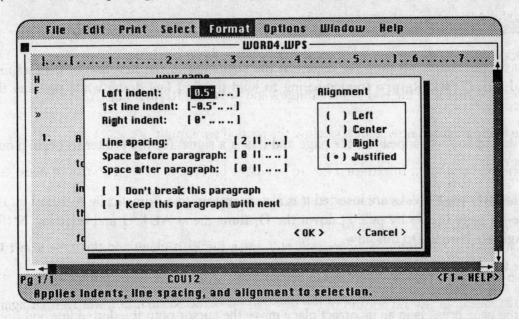

Alter the Left indent to 1" and the Right indent to 1", then **Return** and see the effect.

You can see that the changes have only affected the highlighted paragraph, not the whole text which was the case in the previous session when you changed the **Page Setup & Margins**.

Altering the margins will alter all the text, altering the indents will only affect the highlighted text.

Use **Print Preview** to see the effect.

9. Page breaks

With documents longer than one page, it may be useful for you to decide where you want the printer to start a new page.

Let's say that we want a page break between the first and second paragraphs.

To do this simply position the cursor at the beginning of the first line of paragraph 2 and type **CTRL Return** (remembering to hold the first key down while pressing the second).

A dotted line will appear on the page and this is a signal for the printer to begin a new page.

Whenever page breaks are inserted it is also necessary to automatically re-adjust all the pre-set page breaks by pulling down the **Options** menu **ALT O** and selecting **N** (for **Paginate Now**). Do this now.

Use the **Print Preview** command to see how this would look when printed out.

If the page break is in an incorrect place move the cursor onto the dotted line and press the **Del** key. This will remove the page break and you can then put the break where you want.

Remove the page break and then use the **Print Preview** command to see the revised effect.

10. Printing text

To print the text pull down the **Print** menu and select **P** (for **Print**), then press the **Return** key.

After getting your printout, **Save** your file.

The text should look similar to this:

Your Name

<u>A simple introduction to computing</u>

1   A word-processing program enables the user to

enter text onto the screen, to edit (alter)

the text, to insert new text wherever desired

and to delete text that is unwanted.

Additional features are the formatting of the

text, characters can be in bold, italic, they

can be underlined and paragraphs can be

justified (this means having a straight right

hand margin).

2   Apart from these functions, a **word-processing document** can be

saved (recorded) onto a *<u>floppy or hard disc</u>* and recalled at a

later date. It can then be changed as necessary.

Page 1

37

SESSION 5

Spelling & searching

---

1. Objectives

      By the end of this session you will be able to:

      Use the spellchecker.

      Use the Thesaurus.

      Search and Replace.

---

2. To begin

Open the document file you saved at the end of the last session.

3. Spellchecking

Spellcheckers works in the following way:

There is a dictionary attached to the WORKS program which contains most words in common usage.

The program compares every word in the text with those in the dictionary. If there is a word in the text which is not in the dictionary then WORKS highlights it (this does **not** mean the word is wrong, merely that it does not appear in the dictionary).

Any words not in the dictionary can be added to it for future use.

To use the spellchecker, move to the top of the document by typing **CTRL HOME** and then pull down the **Options** menu (**ALT O**) and select **S** (for **Check Spelling**).

The document is checked and the unknown words appear in the **Dialog box** which is now displayed on screen.

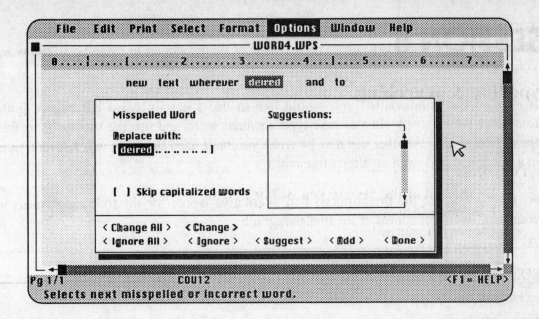

If you like the word and want to keep it just **Return**.

If you want to change it, the command to use is **ALT S** (for **Suggest**). The program will look through the dictionary and suggest any words it can find which are similar to the unknown word.

If one of these is correct, move the cursor onto it and **Return**. The program will then move onto the next unknown word.

If you want to add the word to the dictionary **ALT A** (for **Add**).

If there is no suitable word suggested then type **ALT R** (for **Replace With**) and type the word you want and **Return.**

When the spellchecking has finished, **Return** on **OK**.

Go through the text altering it so that there are six or seven deliberate spelling mistakes. The spellchecker may also discover some non-deliberate ones, let's find out.

4. The thesaurus

The idea of a thesaurus is to give you a choice of words similar in meaning to the word you want to change.

It is often the situation that you would like to use a certain word but cannot quite remember which word. In this case type a similar word and use the thesaurus to find the correct word. Another use may be when you have used the same word several time in a document and want an alternative word.

As an exercise use the thesaurus to find alternative words for the following words in your text, which all appear in the first paragraph.

```
program
text
straight
```

Move the cursor onto the word for which you want an alternative and pull down the **Options menu**.

Select **T** (for **Thesaurus***)* and the alternative words will be displayed.

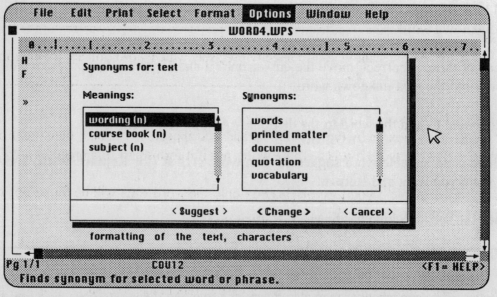

To choose one of these alternatives type **ALT Y** (for **Synonyms**) and move the cursor onto the chosen word, then **Return**.

If none of the words is quite what you are looking for, move the cursor onto the most likely choice and highlight it, then type **ALT S** (for **Suggest***). The program then searches for words similar to that word and so on.

5. Searching for words
It is useful to be able to find a particular word within the text, especially if it extends over several pages.

Before starting to search for a word move the cursor to the beginning of the text (**CTRL HOME**).

Then pull down the **Select** menu (**ALT S**) and from this menu select **Search** by typing **S.**

A dialog box will appear and the first thing to do is to type the word you are searching for.

We are going to search for the word (type the word in lower case).

```
can
```

The other two boxes allow you to specify precisely which word you are looking for:

Match whole word
If you turn this box on by typing **ALT M** and a **X** appears in the box, then the program will only find the word if it is a whole word, not if it forms part of a bigger word.

Using our example if you turn on this box only the word `can` will be found not words like `cannot` or `canned`

Match upper/lowercase
If this box is turned on by typing **ALT U**, the program will only find words which exactly match the mix of upper and lower case letters in the original.

For this example turn on both boxes and **Return**. The first occurrence of the word **can** should be found. Now repeat the search by pressing **F7**, keep doing this until the end of the text.

6. Replace
This works in a similar way to **Search**.

You are going to replace the word

```
text with words
```

To begin, move the cursor to the top of the text and then pull down the **Select** menu.

This time choose **Replace** by typing **R**. The dialog box will appear and you can type the first word (text) you are searching for and then use the **tab** key to move into the next box and type the replacement word (words).

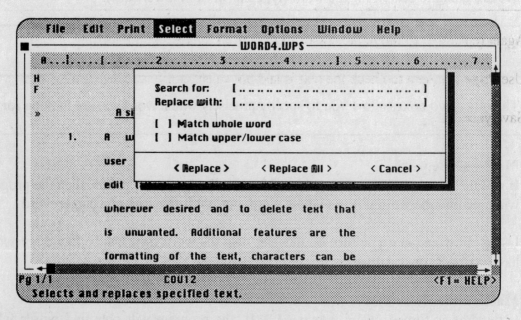

Turn off both boxes (so that they do not contain **X**).

At the bottom of the dialog box you are given a choice of **Replace** or **Replace All**.

If **Replace** is selected then you will be asked each time it is found whether the word is to be replaced.

Replace All replaces all the chosen text without asking you whether you want to.

The default (the automatic choice) is **Replace** and we want to leave this as it is, so just **Return** and follow the prompts that appear so that each time the word `text` appears it is replaced by `words.`

Having successfully done this, now replace the word

```
can
```

with

```
may
```

Again remember to move the cursor to the top of the text before starting.

Use **Page Preview** to check the text is laid out satisfactorily and then print it out.

Save your file.

Session 6

Borders and fonts

---

1. Objectives
By the end of this session you will be able to:
Use borders (boxes around the text).
Change fonts (particular designs and sizes of typefaces).

---

2. To begin
Open the file you saved at the end of the last session.

3. Borders
One of the commands that distinguishes WORKS from older and less sophisticated programs is being able to put borders around selected text. This is very useful for presentation purposes.

You are going to draw a box around the second paragraph of your text.

To do this, highlight the second paragraph, and then pull down the **Format** menu (**ALT T**) and type **O** (for **Borders**). A dialog box will appear.

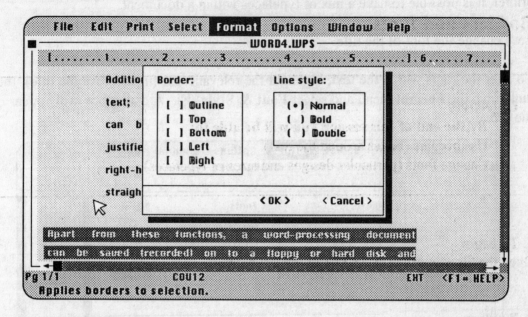

Choose **ALT O** (for **Outline**) and then **ALT N** (for **Normal***)*, then **Return.**   A box will appear around the text.

Now draw a double line style box around paragraph one, make sure that you highlight only the first paragraph and nothing else.

> To remove a box, highlight the text inside the box, and go through the same sequence except to remove all the **X**'s from the border (dialog box), by using **ALT T, ALT M** etc. There should be **nothing** inside the boxes.

To practise, remove the box around paragraph two.

45

4. Fonts

A font is the term for a particular design and size of typeface. Depending upon your printer, it is possible to have a mix of typefaces within a document.

Let's change the font of the title.

To alter the fonts within the text, highlight the relevant text (in this case the title), then pull down the **Format** menu and select **Font & Style** *(F)*. A dialog box will appear on the screen.

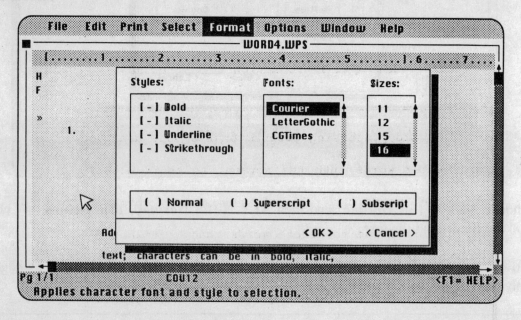

Type **ALT F** (for **Font**) and move the cursor to any of the fonts, highlighting the font you want. Choose any of the available fonts.

Then type **ALT S** (for **Sizes**) and again move the cursor onto the required size. (Choose a larger font size number for this exercise).

When you have completed this press **Return**. The new font does not appear on the screen, only when printed out.

Use **Page Preview** to see the effect and if it is satisfactory, print out the text, although Page Preview does not display the fonts exactly as they appear on the page.

Experiment with the font style and size to see the different effects at your disposal.

Different printers allow widely different font styles and sizes and your lecturer or computer dealer will be able to advise you.

Save your file and quit the program.

Your work should now look similar to this:

Your Name

<u>A simple introduction to computing</u>

1   A word-processing program enables the user to
     enter words onto the screen, to edit (alter)
     the words, to insert new words wherever
     desired and to delete words that is unwanted.
     Additional features are the formatting of the
     words, characters may be in bold, italic,
     they may be underlined and paragraphs may be
     justified (this means having a straight right
     hand margin).

2   Apart from these functions, a **word-processing document** may be
     saved (recorded) onto a _floppy or hard disc_ and recalled at a
     later date. It may then be changed as necessary.

Page 1

SESSION 7

Consolidation

---

1. Objectives
This is a consolidation session to check that you have mastered the program so far. It is not a test of memory, so if you want to, look back over the previous notes or at appendix 2 which contains a summary of the commands covered in the manual.

---

2. Tasks
Load WORKS, open a **NEW** word processing file and type in the following text:

```
The next two parts of the manual contain sessions on the spreadsheet
and database parts of WORKS.

A spreadsheet is used to carry out numeric tasks using the power of
the computer.  One of the advantage of using a spreadsheet is being
able to ask 'What If' questions.  For example what would happen if
the cost of petrol was increased by 20%, how would this affect the
total cost of running a car.  The spreadsheet can be used to
calculate the overall effect of changes to any of the figures in it.

A database is used to organise facts (and figures) in the form of
records.  It is the computer equivalent of a filing cabinet with the
added advantage of being able to look at the records more easily than
if they were kept on paper.
```

Justify the text (give it a straight right hand margin).

Create a title at the top of the text

```
A Look Forward
```

Format the title in bold, italic, underlined and centre it.

Double line space all the text.

Number the paragraphs and use a hanging indent to lay them out.

Alter the margins for all the text to

```
right margin    1"
left margin     2"
```

Add page-numbers to the text and use Page Preview to see the result so far, and if it is satisfactory, print it out.

Move the last two paragraphs around.

Indent the last paragraph so that there is a

```
left indent     1"
first line      -1"
right indent    1"
```

Put a page break between the last two paragraphs.

Spell-check the text.

Replace the word

```
car with motor vehicle
```

Draw a double line box around the last paragraph.

Change the font of the title to a different design and a larger size.

Use Page Preview to check the result and then print and save your file.

Spreadsheets and Charting

With this session we begin to look at the spreadsheet option within WORKS.

So far we have looked at word processing which is concerned with text.

Spreadsheets are concerned with figures and are the computer equivalent of a huge calculator. They enable you to produce anything from a simple calculation through business cash flows to complex budget plans. In fact spreadsheets can be used in any situation that requires calculations using numbers.

Originally all spreadsheet programs could do was carry out mathematic calculations of varying complexity. However business users in particular wanted to display the data in graphs and charts, and Spreadsheet programs now allow you to create graphs and charts easily from the data.

This section of the manual contains the following sessions:

Session 8 Spreadsheets
Session 9 Formulae
Session 10 Layout and Format
Session 11 Editing and sorting
Session 12 Graphs and charts
Session 13 Graphs and formulae
Session 14 Consolidation

The sessions use a simple business example and you will add data and narrative to this as the sessions continue.

SESSION 8

Getting Started

---

1. Objectives

> **By the end of this session you will be able to**:
> Open a spreadsheet file.
> Enter text and values into the spreadsheet.

---

2. Loading the spreadsheet

After WORKS is loaded, the **File** menu is displayed on the screen. Type **N** (for **Create New File**).

Then press **S** (for **New Spreadsheet**).

The spreadsheet screen will appear on the screen.

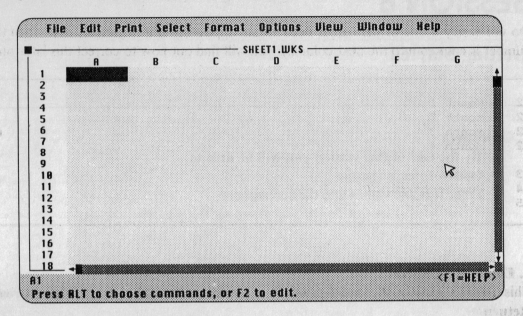

The spreadsheet is made up of **Cells**.

As you can see from the screen the worksheet is made up of a series of **Rows** (across) and **Columns** (down). The **Rows** are numbered **1** to **4096**, and the **Columns** are **A** to **IV**.

The cells you can see at present are called **A1** to **G18**.

You can see in the bottom left of the screen, the letters A1, this identifies the location of the current cell

3. Entering text
The data you are going to enter is based upon the sales made by certain salespersons over a period of several months.

To enter text into a cell, move the cursor to the cell, type the text and press **Return**.

Move the cursor to each of the cells and enter the text (shown below).

Do not worry if one of the names does not all appear (or if it is partially lost when the number is entered into the next column), you will find out how to correct this later on.

```
B2      Month 1
C2      Month 2
D2      Month 3
E2      Month 4

A3      Smith.J
A4      Rumplestskein.Y
A5      Larkins.G
```

4. Entering numbers

This follows exactly the same principle. Move to the cell, type the number and **Return**.

Enter the following:

```
B3      1000
B4      1250        (the last few characters of the name will
                     disappear)
B5       900

C3      1100
C4      1325
C5      1600

D3       900
D4       550
D5       875

E3       780
E4       670
E5       400
```

To finish off this session, put the following title in cell **A1**

```
Salespersons monthly figures
```

It should now look like this:

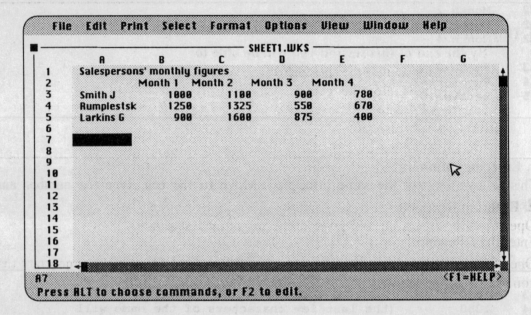

Now save your file (note how it is automatically given a WKS extension, this means it is a WORKS worksheet or spreadsheet file).

SESSION 9

Formulae

---

1. Objectives
    By the end of this session you will be able to:
    Enter formulae into the spreadsheet.
    Copy formula into other cells.
    Use Print Preview.
    Print the spreadsheet.

---

2. Entering formulae

Open the spreadsheet file you saved at the end of the last session.

One of the most important features of a spreadsheet, (and one it is very important that you grasp), is that you can:

get the program to do most of the work

When doing calculations, you instruct the program

how to carry out the calculation

You do **NOT** perform the calculation yourself and then type in the answer

---

The reason for this is that if you enter a formula and then alter any of the figures, the answer will automatically change.

Obviously if you type the answer in, then it will not change automatically when you alter any of the other figures.

Now to instruct the program how to add up the total of the monthly figures for month 1.

a.   Move the cursor to cell **B6**.

b.   Type the = key.

c.   Enter the word (including the bracket).

d.   **SUM(**

e.   Move the cursor onto the cell **B3**.

f.   Enter a   :   (this means a colon symbol)

g.   Move the cursor to cell **B5**

(this should highlight cells B3 to B5).

h.   Close the brackets and **return**. The answer will then appear.

The formula should look like this:

=sum(B3:B5)

This means you are adding up
all the cells between B3 and B5

Now add up the totals for the other months.

Finally enter a formula into cell **F3** to add up the total for Smith.

3. Copying formula

Rather then having to enter formulae into every cell, a spreadsheet allows you to copy the **formula**, into other cells.

It is important to realise that you are **NOT** copying the figure which appears on the screen, but the underlying formula you have entered into the cell you are copying.

You can now copy the formula you have entered into **F3** into cells **F4** to **F6**.

To do this:

Move the cursor into the cell you want to copy (in this case **F3**).

Press the **Extend** key (**F8**) and move the cursor onto cell **F6**. You should see that all the cells from **F3** to **F6** have now been highlighted.

Pull down the **Edit** menu and select **F** (for **Fill Down**).

The formula has now been copied and the answers have appeared in the cells **F4** to **F6**.

4. Recalculation

The WORKS spreadsheet automatically recalculates the answers when any of the figures are altered.

Move to the cell **C4** and enter the figure **9999**. You can see that the relevant answers (in cells **C6**, **F4** and **F6**) have changed.

Change the figure in **C4** back to **1325** and again see how the program automatically changes the answers.

Now add the following text into the cells to add explanation to the chart.

```
A6    Total
F2    Total
```

---

5. Print preview
This operates in the same way as with the word-processing section:

Pull down the **Print** menu.

Select **V** (for **Preview**), followed by **ALT P** and when you have finished looking at it, **ESC** to get back to the spreadsheet.

If the spreadsheet does not fit on to a single page, pull down the **Format** menu by selecting **ALT T** (for **Format**), **F** (for **Font**) and **ALT S** (for **Size**) and highlight a smaller number, then **Return.**

Use **Page Preview** again to see if it will fit.

---

6. Printing the spreadsheet
Pull down the **Print** menu.

Select **P** (for **Print**) and **Return**.

Now save the file.

SESSION 10

Layout and format

---

1. Objectives
   By the end of this session you will be able to:
   Insert rows and columns.
   Delete rows and columns.
   Alter column width.
   Format cells.

---

2. Inserting rows and columns

Load Works and your spreadsheet file from the previous session.

It is often necessary to insert additional information into a spreadsheet by inserting more rows or columns.

You are going to insert an additional Row and Column to make more space (so that the spreadsheet is easier to read).

Move the cursor to cell **A2**.

Pull down the **Edit** menu and select **I** for (**Insert Row/Column**).

A new dialog box will appear, from this you can select **Rows** or **Columns** by typing **R** or **C**. Since **R** is already selected just **Return**.

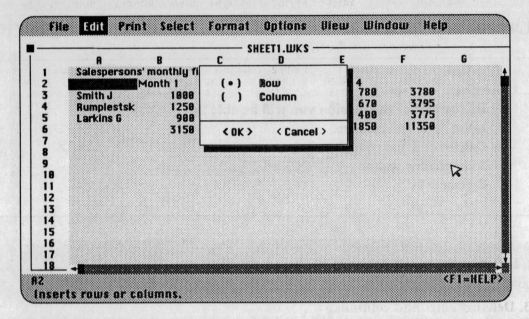

An additional Row should now appear (note how the other Rows move down to compensate).

Now add an additional Column in Column **F**. Remember to move the cursor into column **F** before starting and choose **C** (for **Columns**) in the dialog box.

Your screen should look like this:

File	Edit	Print	Select	Format	Options	View	Window	Help

SHEET1.WKS

	A	B	C	D	E	F	G
1	Salespersons' monthly figures						
2							
3		Month 1	Month 2	Month 3	Month 4		Total
4	Smith J	1000	1100	900	780		3780
5	Rumplestsk	1250	1325	550	670		3795
6	Larkins G	900	1600	875	400		3775
7	Total	3150	4025	2325	1850		11350
8							
9							
10							
11							
12							
13							
14							
15							
16							
17							
18							

f3   <F1=HELP>

Press ALT to choose commands, or F2 to edit.

3. Deleting rows and columns
If you have made a mistake or just want to remove a row or column then:

Move the cursor into the column or row you want to delete and then pull down the **Edit** menu.

Select **D** for (**Delete Row/Column**), then choose **R** or **C** and **Return**.

Remove the blank Column **F** (**after having Saved your file**).

It is very important to save a file before deleting anything, because if you delete the wrong data then you have lost it!

4. Altering column width

The width of the cells is set at 10 characters. For various reasons it may be desirable to change the column width for example the column heading may exceed the normal column width.

You are going to change the width of the total column **F**.

Move the cursor to column **F**.

Then pull down the **Format** menu and select **W** (for **Column Width**).

Type a number representing the chosen column width, in this case **12** and **Return.**
Now alter the width of column **A** to **19** characters, you can now see that all the names appear (without any of them being cut off).

Insert an additional Row just below **Smith** and add the following, **remember** to move the cursor to Row 5 first.

```
A5      Carter.M
B5        600
C5        800
D5       1000
E5        300
```

Copy the formula in **F4** into **F5**.

See how all the answers have changed to take account of the additional data.

Your work should look like this:

```
 File   Edit   Print   Select   Format   Options   View   Window   Help
 ■─────────────────────── SHEET1.WKS ───────────────────────
        A         B          C          D          E          F
   1   Salespersons' monthly figures
   2
   3              Month 1    Month 2    Month 3    Month 4    Total
   4   Smith J       1000       1100        900        780      3780
   5   Carter M       600        800       1000        300      2700
   6   Rumplestskein Y 1250      1325        550        670      3795
   7   Larkins G      900       1600        875        400      3775
   8   Total         3750       4825       3325       2150     14050
   9
  10
  11
  12
  13
  14
  15
  16
  17
  18
 C12                                                        <F1=HELP>
 Press ALT to choose commands, or F2 to edit.
```

5. Formatting cells

Besides altering the width of cells you may want to change the format. For example you may want to alter how numbers are displayed (number of decimal places, £ signs etc.), or whether the text should be aligned to the left, centre or to the right.

To begin you are going to format the total figures in column **F** to display £ signs.

Firstly highlight the figures you want to Format, in this case the figures in column F.

Then pull down the **Format** menu, select **U** (for **Currency**) and enter **0** as the number of decimal places.

Then **Return** and the cells will be displayed with £ signs and no decimal places.

Do the same with the totals along the bottom of the worksheet (Row **8**).

Now you are going to format the titles along the top of the worksheet (Row **3**):

Highlight the cells, pull down the **Format** menu and select **S** (for **Style**).

A dialog box will appear on the screen.

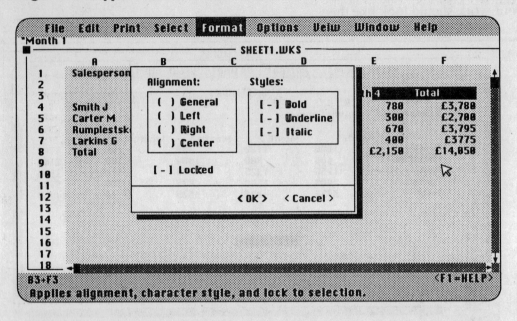

Type **ALT R** (for **Right**), **ALT U** (for **Underline**) and **ALT B** (for **Bold**), then **Return**.

The titles along the top will now be aligned to the right, underlined and in bold.

If this has not worked, check whether you did in fact highlight all the cells you wanted to format **before** pulling down the **Format** menu

---

Now format the title **(A1)** to **Italic**, **Underlined**, and the names of the salesmen in Column **A** so that they are in both **Bold** and **Italic**.

Add an empty Row so that the totals in Row **8** move down to Row **9**.

Your work should now look like this:

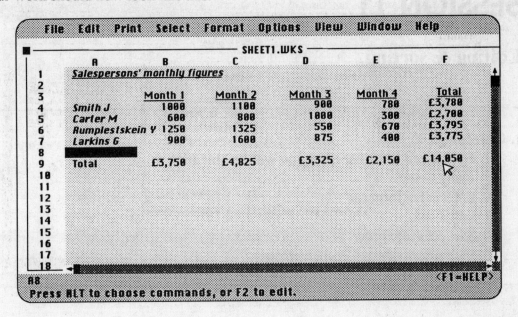

Save the file.

SESSION 11

Editing & sorting

---

1. Objectives

    By the end of this session you will be able to:

Blank Cells.

Enter other formulae.

Edit a cell.

Sort cells into order.

Multiply, divide and do percentages.

---

2. Blanking cells

Firstly load WORKS and open the previous worksheet.

To blank a cell or cells, highlight the cells concerned and pull down the **Edit** menu.

To see how this works, highlight the cells **C4** and **C5** (together), then

Pull down the **Edit** menu.

Select **E** (for **Clear**) and the contents of the cell will be removed.

Type these new figures into the blank cells and notice how the totals are automatically recalculated.

C4	200
C5	150

---

3. Entering other formulae
So far you have entered formula to add cells up.

Other mathematic expressions are allowed for example dividing and multiplying, as well as many functions (e.g. **SUM, AVG** etc).

Add the following data to the worksheet:

Remember to copy the 2500 rather than type it in four times (by highlighting and **Filling Right**).

```
A10     Minimum sales
A11     Sales less minimum

B10     2500
C10     2500
D10     2500
E10     2500
```

To calculate the figures for Row **11**, move the cursor to **B11** and type the = sign (this is the symbol used to start a calculation).

Move the cursor to cell **B9** and then type a - sign, then move the cursor to **B10** and press **Return.**

The formula will read:

   =B9-B10

Now copy the formula into cells **C11** to **E11**.

> Your work should look similar to this:

```
 File   Edit   Print   Select   Format   Options   View   Window   Help
■────────────────────────── SHEET1.WKS ──────────────────────
        A          B          C          D          E          F
 1   Salespersons' monthly figures
 2
 3                  Month 1    Month 2    Month 3    Month 4     Total
 4   Smith J         1000        200        900        780      £2,880
 5   Carter M         600        150       1000        300      £2,050
 6   Rumplestskein Y 1250       1325        550        670      £3,795
 7   Larkins G        900       1600        875        400      £3,775
 8
 9   Total          £3,750     £3,275     £3,325     £2,150    £12,500
10   Minimum sales   2500       2500       2500       2500
11   sales less minimum 1250     775        825       -350
12
13
14
15
16
17
18
A13                                                          <F1=HELP>
Press ALT to choose commands, or F2 to edit.
```

4. Tidying up the worksheet

Format cells **A10** and **A11** to italic and underlined.

Format the figures in Rows **10** and **11** to display £ signs but no decimal places.

5. Editing a cell

It is useful to be able to alter the contents of a cell without retyping it.

To do this move the cursor to the cell and press the **F2** key. The cell contents will be displayed in the upper left of the worksheet.

Use the cursor keys (or the mouse) to move around the contents displayed and alter them as necessary. To practise, alter the contents of the cells

```
A4 to Smother.J
A9 to Total Sales
D7 to 975
```

6. Sorting cells into order

You are now going to re-arrange the names of the salesmen into alphabetic order, to do this:

Highlight cells **A4** to **F7**, this defines the range you want to sort.

(if you had highlighted the whole spreadsheet then the totals, etc. would have been included in the sorting !)

Pull down the **Select** menu (**ALT S**) and from this **O** (for **Sort rows**).

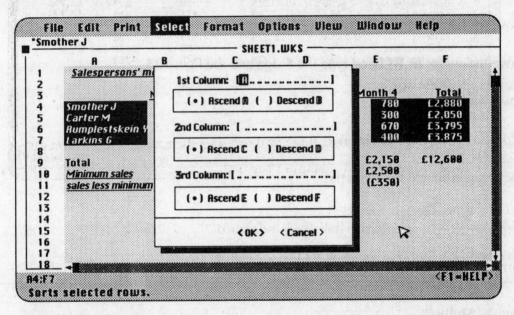

The 1st (and only) column you are sorting is **A** (alter this if need be) and **Return.**

You can see that the highlighted rows have been sorted into alphabetic order of name and that the rest of the data has been carried with the names.

7. Multiplying and dividing

Add the following data to the worksheet:

A13   Commission

Format cell **A13** to italic and bold.

Now to calculate the commission payable as 25% of the figure in cell **A11**.

Move the cursor to cell **B13** and press the = sign.

Move the cursor to **B11** and type the * sign and the figure **25**.

Now type the / sign.

Type the figure **100** and **Return**.

The formula should look like this:

> **=B11*25/100**

This means multiply the figure in **B11** by 25 and divide by 100.

---

* means Multiply
/ means Divide

Copy the formula in **B13** from **C13** to **E13**.

Format the cells **B13** to **E13** to **Currency** with no decimal places.

Save your file.

Your final worksheet should look like this.

	File	Edit	Print	Select	Format	Options	View	Window	Help

SHEET1.WKS

	A	B	C	D	E	F
1	*Salespersons' monthly figures*					
2						
3		Month 1	Month 2	Month 3	Month 4	Total
4	*Carter M*	600	150	1000	300	£2,050
5	*Larkins G*	900	1600	975	400	£3,875
6	*Rumplestskein Y*	1250	1325	550	670	£3,795
7	*Larkins G*	1000	200	900	780	£2,880
8						
9	Total	£3,750	£3,275	£3,425	£2,150	£13,570
10	*Minimum sales*	£2,500	£2,500	£2,500	£2,500	
11	*sales less minimum*	£1,250	£775	£925	(£350)	
12						
13	Commission	£313	£194	£231	(£88)	
14						
15						
16						
17						
18						

A15

<F1=HELP>

Press ALT to choose commands, or F2 to edit.

SESSION 12

Graphs and charts

---

1. Objectives
> **This session deals with drawing graphs and charts from the spreadsheet figures. By the end of this session you will be able to**:
> Draw a simple bar chart.
> Add a title.
> Display legends.
> Print the chart.
> Add grid lines to a bar chart.
> Draw a stacked bar chart.
> Alter the font of the title.

---

2. To begin
Open the spreadsheet file you saved in the last session.

3. Drawing a bar chart
Highlight the cells **A3** to **F7** only.

Pull down the **View** menu.

Select **N** (for **New Chart**).

Press the **ESC** key when you have finished looking at your chart.

Now you can add additional information to the chart so that the reader can understand the chart more easily.

4. Adding titles to a chart

Pull down the **Data** menu and select **T** (for **Titles**). The following screen will appear:

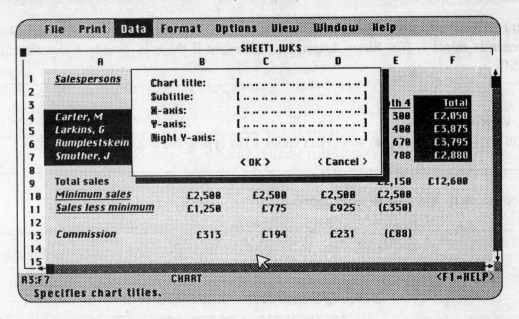

Enter in the Chart Title box

```
Salesmens figures
```

and in the Subtitle box

```
for four months -  by your name
```

Don't worry about the text disappearing to the left, it will all appear on the chart.

Enter in the Y-axis box

```
pounds
```

and **Return**.

5. Displaying legends
It is often useful to show on the graph what each of the bars represent:

Pull down the **Options** menu and if there is **no** dot in front of the command **Show Legends** select **L** (for **Show Legends**), otherwise if there is already a dot then just **ESC**.

6. Viewing the chart
Pull down the **View** menu and select Chart 1 (by typing the character **1**).

Your chart should look similar to this:

Salesmens figures
for four months - by your name

Legend:
- Carter.M
- Rumplestskein.Y
- Larkins.G
- Smother.J

7. Adding grid lines to a graph
Grid lines are the horizontal or vertical rules on the chart to which show more clearly the value of the lines drawn.

To draw grid lines:

Pull down the **Options** menu and select **Y** (for **Y-axis**)

Turn on the **Grid box** by typing **ALT G** (when a box is turned on an **X** will appear in the box) and then **Return**.

Now view the graph again to see the effect of the grid lines.

8. Drawing a stacked bar chart
To change the type of chart pull down the **Format** menu and select S (for **Stacked bar chart**).

Then view the chart to see how a stacked bar chart appears.

9. Altering the font of the title
To alter the font means to change the size and typeface (design) of the characters. To do this:

Pull down the **Format** menu and select **F** (for **Title Font**).

A dialog box will appear, move the cursor to one of the Fonts highlighting the one you decide on.

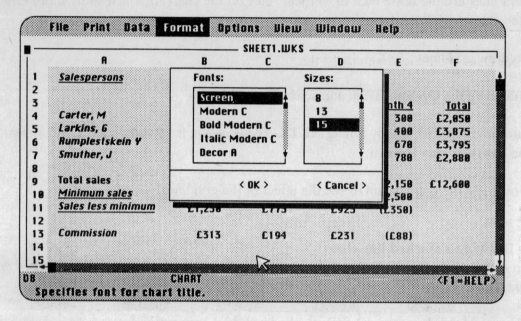

Type **ALT S** (for **Size**) and move the cursor to the largest number again highlighting it and **return**.

Remember that the range and size of fonts is determined by your printer, so experiment to find a suitable one.

Now change the font for the other text by the same method, so this time select **O** (for **Other Fonts**) and choose a Font and a small font size.

To display the new font on the screen, pull down the **Options** menu and check whether the command

Show printer fonts

has been selected, it will have a dot in front of it if it has. It there is no dot, type **S**.

Pull down the **Print** menu and select **Preview**. If this is satisfactory, print the chart.

Save the file.

Your chart should look similar to this:

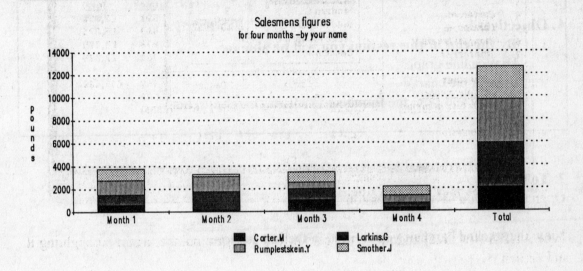

SESSION 13

Graphs and formulae

---

1. Objectives
   By the end of this session you will be able to:
   Draw a line graph.
   Draw a pie chart.
   Display and print the formulae.

---

2. To begin
Open the file you saved last session.

View the stacked barchart you created in the last session.

3. Drawing line graphs
Once the first type of graph has been created, all that is needed to change to another type of graph is to:

Pull down the **Format** menu and select the type of graph you want to draw, in this case select:

L (for Line)

Then **View** the chart, you now have a line graph instead of the bar chart.

If the legend (the explanation of what each colour represents) is not shown below the horizontal axis, then simply pull down pull down the **Options** menu and if there is **no** dot in front of the word **legend** select **L** (for **Legend**), if there is already a dot then just **ESC**.

---

4. Creating a pie chart

If you want to create a new chart (for example to chart a different range of figures from the same spreadsheet) then you need to begin the process again by firstly:

Highlighting the cells in the spreadsheet you want to include in the chart.

For this task highlight cells **F4** to **F7** (the total figures for each salesman).

Then pull down the **View** menu and select **N** (for **New**).

Pull down the **Format** menu and choose **P** (for **Pie**).

Finally look at the chart by pulling down the **View** menu again and selecting the chart you want to see.

(normally this will be the bottom chart, the charts are listed in order you produced them).

A pie chart will appear on the screen and will show the total figures with the % each represents of the total.

5. Adding text to the pie chart

So that the person looking at the chart can be given more information you may need to add explanations to the chart.

To do this highlight the cells you want as labels (**A4** to **A7**).

Pull down the **Data** menu and select **X** (for **X-series**).

Then **View** the chart again and the salesmens names appear next to their segments of the chart.

Now add the following title to the chart:

```
Salesmens totals for four months
```

and a subtitle

```
by your name
```

Now alter the **Title font** to make it bigger and alter the **Other Fonts** to make them smaller.

Pull down the **Print** menu and select **Preview**. If this looks correct then print your chart.

The chart should be similar to this:

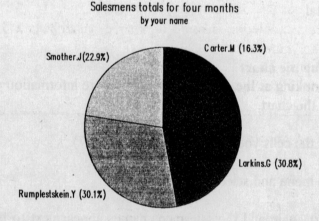

Salesmens totals for four months
by your name

Smother.J (22.9%)

Carter.M (16.3%)

Larkins.G (30.8%)

Rumplestskein.Y (30.1%)

Save your file.

SESSION 14

Consolidation

<hr>

1. Objectives.
This session consolidates the material from the spreadsheet sessions. If you are unsure
how to carry out a specific operation, look back over the sessions. The tasks in this
session are given in the same sequence as they were covered in the individual sessions.
Also you can refer to appendix 2.

<hr>

Tasks

1.   Load WORKS.

2.   Open a **New** Spreadsheet file.

3.   The data you are entering is based on a shop which buys and sells cuddly toy
        dogs, bears and hippos.

        Enter the data in a table as shown below:

<hr>

```
Profit analysis by product
by your name

Product             Cost                Sell at         Profit
Dogs                8.41                10.35
Bears               3.65                 5.67
Hippos              9.99                12.87
```

<hr>

4.   Enter a formula for the profit (sell at minus cost) for Dogs and then copy the
        formula down into the two cells below.

5.   The company is considering adding another product to its range:

```
Lions  cost    5.55           sell at    7.32
```

Add this to the worksheet between Dogs and Bears and enter a formula for the profit, by copying it from the cell above.

6.   Format the worksheet as necessary to make all the data as presentable as possible (for example the headings over the figures should be right aligned above the figures).

7.   Pull down the Print menu and Preview the worksheet, if it is satisfactory, print it out.

8.   Format the cells with numbers in them to show £ signs and 2 decimal places.

9.   Format the headings (Product, Cost etc.) so that they are underlined and format the names of the animals in italic.

10   Insert a column at the left of the worksheet (column **A**) and enter the following new data into it (you need to position the data to line up with the rest of the rows already there).

```
Number
       3
       2
       4
       6
Total
```

The words Number and Total should be underlined.

11.   Centre the figures in column A.

12.   Then put a new heading to the right of Profit called

```
Total
```

and underline it and format it to the right.

13.   Enter a formula to calculate total (number*profit) and copy this down into the next three cells.

14.   Add up the total of this column by using the SUM formula.

15.   Format this column to show pounds signs and 2 decimal places.

16.   Sort the rows containing the animals names into alphabetic order.

17.   Print Preview the worksheet and Print it (make sure it all fits onto one page by altering the fonts as necessary).

18.   Draw a bar chart with heading, subheading and a legend after highlighting the data in the **product, cost, sell at and profit columns only** (include the titles for these columns).

19.   Add a suitable title and subtitle to the graph making sure you include your own name somewhere. Also name the Y axis.

20.   Alter the font for the title (and for the other text) to give the most effective layout.

21.   Add horizontal grid lines to the chart and print it out after having previewed it.

The finished result should look similar to this:

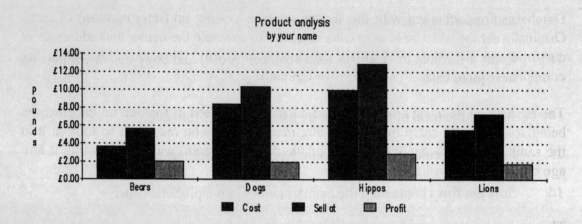

Save your file and quit the program.

Databases

This is the first session concerned with the database part of the WORKS program.

Databases are concerned with the storing and the looking up (interrogation) of facts. Originally data used to be kept in card indexes, for example the names and addresses of customers or the records of all the employees in a firm. Nowadays businesses use computerised databases to keep this kind of data.

The advantages of using a computerised database are speed of looking up information, being able to easily share the data among many people who may wish to look at it at the same time and being able to look at the data in different ways, e.g. sorting it into age or department order.

This section of the manual contains the following:

Session 15 Databases
Session 16 Searching
Session 17 Reports

SESSION 15

Getting Started

---

1. Objectives
> **By the end of this session you will be able to**:
> Open a database file.
> Create a file structure.
> Enter data onto the record cards.
> Add data to a file.
> Sort a datafile into order.

---

2. How a database is organized

Before you can begin to create a database file, you have to have an understanding of how a database is organized.

Consider a card index where **records** are kept of employees in a firm.

Each employee would have their own **record card** and all the records together would be called a **File**.

Each **record** would contain certain data, for example the employees name, address, age and so on.

Each item in a record is called a **field**, so in our example each **record** would contain a name **field**, an address **field** and so on.

Exactly the same terms are used with a computerised database which in its simplest form is a computerised card index.

Thus a computer database consists of:

A File (there may be several files e.g. an employee file, a stock file etc).

Each file is divided into **Records** (e.g. each employee or stock type will have its own record).

Each record is divided into fields according to the type of information held in the record.

3. To begin creating a database file
Choose **Create New file** and then open a **New Database**.

A blank form will appear on the screen.

4. Creating a file structure
You are going to create a customer database for Perfect Pets Ltd.

To start you need to create a **FORM**. This may look just like a handwritten record card.

Enter the following label at the top of the form and **Return.**

```
Customer record
```

Then while the title is highlighted, pull down the **Format** menu and select **S** (for **Style**).

Choose bold, underlined and italic.

5. To enter field names on to the FORM

Move the cursor to the required position (look at the example later in this session to get an idea of the layout) and type the **Field** Name (this must have a colon : as the final character and may contain spaces).

Use the cursor keys to move down and/or across the form.

Return after typing the **Field** name and accept the given **Width** and **Height** (by **Returning**).

Enter the following field names:

```
Customer name :
Address 1 :
Address 2 :
Address 3 :
Postcode :
Contact :
Phone No :
```

When finished your screen may look like this:

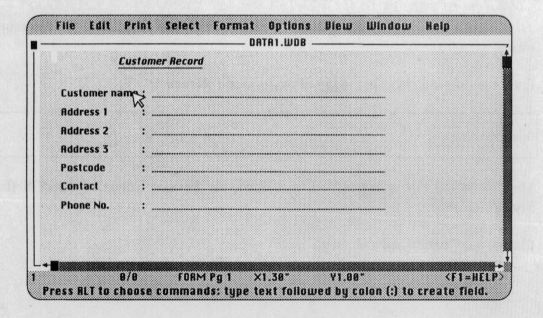

6. Altering the design of the form
If after creating your form you do not like the layout or you want to edit the fieldnames then:

To move the fieldname
Highlight the fieldname, pull down the **Edit** menu and type **M** (for **Move**).

Move the cursor to the new position and **Return**, this will move the fieldname to the new position.

To edit the fieldname
Highlight the fieldname.

F2 is the edit key and if you press F2 you can edit the text which is then displayed in the top left of the screen.

To adjust the length of the fieldname
Move the cursor underneath the colon **:** sign and press the spacebar as many times as necessary to line up all the field names as shown below.

To insert or delete lines
To insert or delete lines in your form, select **Edit** and **Insert / Delete lines** (remember to position the cursor first).

---

7. Entering data on to the form
The **Form** will displayed on the screen ready for you to enter the data into each field.

After entering data into a field use the **TAB** key to move to the next field and at the end of the record on to the next record.

To move back up the record use **Shift Tab**.

Enter the following data:

```
Jeremiah Josephs
The Croft
Ravensbourne
Cumbria
KN34 6TY
Ms Kunnop
0876-234512

Toytown for Toddlers
Trentown
Blandford
Dorset
SA11 5RT
Mr Tonkins
0546-23-5675

Kiddies Korner
Keytown
Birmingham
West Midlands
BM55 7FR
Mrs Rawlings
066-65-3987

Tamleys
Short Street
Regents Park
London
SW1 4CD
Mr Jones
071-234-6598
```

Return after the final item.

8. Looking at the data another way
WORKS allows you to look at the data as a **Form** and as a **List.**

To look at the data as a **List:**

Pull down the **View** menu and type **L** (for **List**) and **CTRL HOME** to move the cursor to the first record.

The problem now is that the field widths are too narrow to display the data, and it seems jumbled.

You need to widen certain of the fields to display the data more clearly.

To do this, move to the first field, pull down the **Format** menu and select **W** (for **Field Width**), enter the required number of characters (as shown below) and **Return**.

```
        Customer name :    22
        Address 1 :        13
        Address 2 :        13
        Address 3 :        14
        Postcode :         10
        Contact :          13
        Phone No :         14
```

Now that the fields have been widened it is not possible to see all the data on the screen at the same time, so you need to use the **Cursor, Home** and **End** keys to move around the file.

9. Returning to Form View
Pull down the **View** menu and select **F** (for **Form**).

By pulling down the **View** menu and selecting the screen you want you can alternate between **List** and **Form**.

10. Adding records to the datafile
To add records to a file make sure that the **Form** is on the screen.

If the **List** screen is displayed (i.e. the records are shown across the screen rather than down the screen) then

Pull down the **View** menu and select **F** for (**Form**).

To enter a new record type **CTRL END** (this moves the cursor to the next blank record).

Enter the following new data (after moving the cursor to the first field in the blank record):

```
Simply Super
Blackdown
Verwood
Dorset
DT23 7HT
Ms Nettles
0786-23519

Yourname
The Old Shop
Blandford
Dorset
DT51 8KJ
Mr Jones
0953-23497
```

After entering this pull down the **View** menu and type **L** (for **List**).

Then **CTRL HOME** to move the cursor to the top.

You should see the new items appearing at the bottom of the display.

11. Sorting the datafile into order

Since the data is usually not entered in alphabetic or numeric order it is necessary at times to sort the file into a particular order.

This can be done at any time and the file can be sorted in any way you wish, for example you can sort the file into alphabetic order by customer.

To do this make sure that the **List** display is on screen (the records are shown across the screen).

Then move the cursor to the customer name field.

Pull down the **Select** menu and type **O** (for **Sort Records**). At this point your screen should look like this:

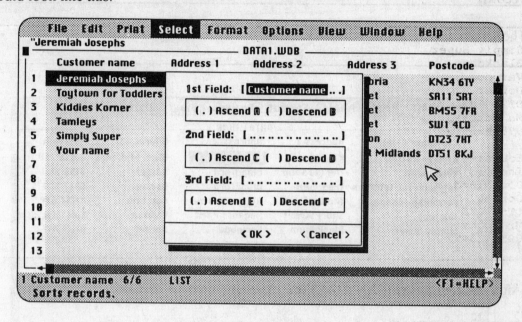

The **Customer Name** should appear in the first field in the dialog box, make sure that **Ascending** has been selected and **Return**.

The file should now display the data sorted into ascending order of customer name.

---

note that the data in all the other fields is carried with the sorted field

---

Now to practise, sort the data into **descending** order of **Customer Name.**

You can sort on any field so now sort the file into ascending order of **Address 2** (the town) and see how the data has been reorganized.

If the wrong Field Name is displayed in the dialog box then overtype it with the correct one, i.e. the one you want to sort by.

---

databases

Save the file.

The screen display should now look similar to this:

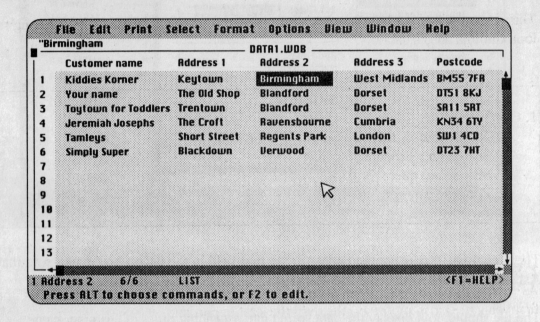

SESSION 16

Searching

This session will cover how to extract information from the database without having to look through all the data.

---

1. Objectives
> **By the end of this session you will be able to:**
> Search on more than one field.
> Search and query for data.
> Print the data.

---

2. Sorting on more than one field
As well as sorting on one field, WORKS enables you to sort on up to three fields, the first being the most important, the third the least important.

Open your datafile and pull down the **Select** menu and choose **Sort Records**.

Type **Address 3** in the first field , and type **Address 2** in the second field and **Return** after making sure you have selected **ASCENDING**.

Now look at the data, it is ordered firstly in alphabetic order of **Address 3**.

Then look closely at the **Address 2** field, it has been sorted into alphabetic order **within Address 3**, so that within **Dorset**, the towns in **Address 2** have been put into alphabetic order.

> The display should look like this:

```
 File  Edit  Print  Select  Format  Options  View  Window  Help
 "Birmingham                         DATA1.WDB
■    Customer name      Address 1      Address 2      Address 3      Postcode
 1   Jeremiah Josephs   The Croft      Ravensbourne   Cumbria        KN34 6TY
 2   Your name          The Old Shop   Blandford      Dorset         DT51 8KJ
 3   Toytown for Toddlers Trentown     Blandford      Dorset         SA11 5RT
 4   Simply Super       Blackdown      Verwood        Dorset         DT23 7HT
 5   Tamleys            Short Street   Regents Park   London         SW1 4CD
 6   Kiddies Korner     Keytown        Birmingham     West Midlands  BM55 7FR
 7
 8
 9
10
11
12
13
13 Address 1    6/6       LIST                                    <F1=HELP>
     Press ALT to choose commands, or F2 to edit.
```

3. Searching for specific data

Make sure you are showing the **List** screen (with the records across the screen).

Pull down the **View** menu and select **Query.**

Type the data you are looking for in the relevant fields, in this case type:

> Dorset   in the **Address 3** field and **Return**

then press **F10** to see the data conforming to this query displayed on the screen.

Now search for all the Customer names beginning with a **T**, carry out a similar search (just enter **T*** in the relevant field after deleting the data from the previous search).

4. Using wildcards

Note how you used the * symbol in the last search, this symbol is called a **wildcard**, and means any characters. Thus * on its own would mean any data in that field.

Putting a * after a letter or letters narrows the search (for example T* means any name beginning with the letter T).

5. Entering more than one search condition

Now enter the following additional data to the search (this time leave the T* in the customer name field)

D*   in the **Address 3** field and **return**

Then **F10** to see the result of the search. The screen will display those records that have a **customer name field** beginning with T **and** which have an **address 3 field** beginning with D

6. Other types of search conditions

As well as those shown above you can make other types of conditions for your search:

<>	not equal to
>	greater then
<	less than
>=	greater than or equal to

these can be used with numbers **or** letters, if they are used with letters then the letters **have** to be in speech marks.

for example   <>"T*"   will list all those records **not** starting with the letter **T**

Now, search for all those customers where the customer name does **not** begin with a T. Remember to delete the original search conditions first

7. Printing the records

Delete all the search conditions.

Pull down the **View** menu and type **L** (for **List**).

All six records should appear on the screen.

Pull down the **View** menu and select **Form**.

Now pull down the **Print** menu, select **Print** and you will see there are more questions than usual in the dialog box.

Check that the **page breaks** box is turned **off** (there should **not** be any symbol in the box, if there is type **ALT B** to remove it).

Enter 0.2 inches for the space between records.

Check the **All records** box has a dot in front of it, if not type **ALT A** to select it.

Do the same with the **All Items** box (this should also be selected to show a dot).

Then **Return** and the data will be printed out.

Save the file.

SESSION 17

Reports

In this session you will learn how to create a report based upon the data held in the datafile.

A report allows you to decide exactly how to lay out the data and not to be limited to how it is shown in either the **Form** or **List** screen displays.

---

1. Objectives

> **By the end of this session you will be able to**:
> Create a report.
> Change the character fonts.
> Add to the report.
> Print the report.

---

2. Reports
Open your database file you saved at the end of the last session.

Pull down the **View** menu and then select **N** (for **New report**).

WORKS displays a report containing the data in your database file.

Press **Return** to move through the report until you get to the last screen, which looks like this:

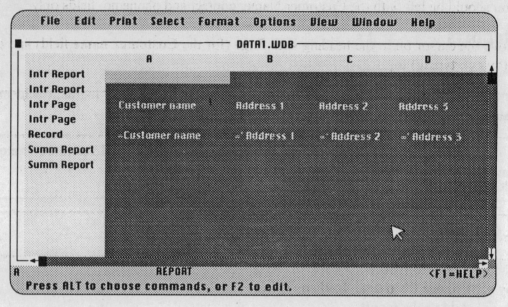

This screen allows you to:

> add titles
> alter the column labels (names)
> change the width
> format the cells
> enter the date
> remove or rearrange the columns

Add the following title to the report (in the row **Intr Report**):

```
Customer contacts
```

then remove all the **address** columns in columns **B**, **C** and **D** by moving the cursor onto each and pulling down the **Edit** menu

and selecting **D** (for **Delete**) and **C** (for **Column**), then **Return**.

Do the same for the **postcode** field.

You should be left with the Customer Name, contact and phone no. fields only.

Move the cursor on to the heading **Intr Page** (for the **Customer name** field) and alter it (by overtyping) to:

```
Name
```

Alter the **Phone no** heading to:

```
Phone
```

(by editing, use **F2** and the **backspace** key).

Pull down the **View** menu and select the report (it should be called **Report 1**).

The screen display should look like this:

```
Customer contacts

Name                        Contact        Phone

Jeremiah Josephs            Ms Kunnop      0876-234512
Your name                   Mr Jones       0953-23497
Toytown for Toddlers        Mr Tonkins     0546-23-5675
Simply Super                Ms Nettles     0786-23519
Tamleys                     Mr Jones       071-234-6598
Kiddies Korner              Mrs Rawlings   066-65-3987




Page 1                      REPORT                         <F1=HELP>
  Press ENTER to continue, ESC to cancel.
```

Then **ESC** back to the **Report Form** when you have finished

3. Changing character styles

You can alter the formatting of the **report** to make certain items stand out and to make the report look more professional.

Move the cursor on to the main title Customer Contacts.

Pull down the **Format** menu and select **Style**. Choose bold, underline and italic and **Return**.

Highlight the column labels (headings) and format these (together) so that they are underlined and in italic.

4. Entering the date into the report

Move the cursor to the cell below the title and enter the current date by typing the **CTRL** key and while holding this type the **;** key as well.

then **Return**, this will enter the date into that cell.

Format the date to show to the **left** of the cell by pulling down the **Format** menu and selecting **S** (for **Style**).

5. Adding additional text to the report

Move the cursor into the first column, to the bottom row **(Summ Report)** and enter the following:

```
A list of our customer contacts
```

Now view the finished report and **ESC** when finished.

6. Printing the report

Pull down the **Print** menu and select **Preview.**

Look at your report and if it looks satisfactory, print it out.

Save your file and quit the program.

Using MS Works in an integrated way

Now you have understood how to deal with the individual parts of the program, you will learn how to integrate them, for example how to produce reports with text, figures from the spreadsheet and graphs in it. This really uses the power and facilities available in an integrated program like MS Works and lets you produce very professional results.

You will make use of some of the material you have already created as well as creating some new files.

The contents in this section are:

Session 18 Integrating Word Processed and Spreadsheet files
Session 19 Mailmerging
Session 20 Final exercise - incorporating spreadsheets, word processing and databases

SESSION 18

Integrating Word Processed and Spreadsheet Files

---

1. Objectives

> **By the end of this session you will be able to**:
> Combine a word processed document with figures from a spreadsheet.
> Incorporate a spreadsheet chart into a report.

---

2. To start

Open a **New** word-processing file.

Type the following text, making sure you justify **and** spellcheck the text.

```
To:   Fred Jones
Dept: Marketing

From: Sally Buttons
Dept: Sales
                        Memo
I am sending you the figures showing the profit projections for our
products, these are to be distributed to the retail customers to show
them how profitable it is to buy and resell these items.

I suggest you mailmerge the customers with this information.
```

Now save your file.

3. Copying figures from the spreadsheet
Move the cursor to the position in the document you want the figures to appear (in this case below the text).

Open the spreadsheet file you saved for **Perfect Pets** (from session 14).

Pull down the **View** menu and select **S** (for **Spreadsheet**) and highlight **all** the figures and text.

Pull down the **Edit** menu and select **C** (for **Copy**).

Type **CTRL F6** to move back to the word processed document (or use the **Window menu** and select the file).

Check the position of the cursor and press **Return**.

This will copy the spreadsheet figures into the document.

Use the **return** key to insert spaces if necessary between the text and the figures (remove any unnecessary underlining).

You can see that the figures may not be laid out very satisfactorily: the last column has wrapped around. The reason for this is that the page margins are not wide enough.

To widen the margins within the word processor, pull down the **Print** menu and select **M** (for **Page setup & margins**)

Alter the right margin to 0.5 inches and the left margin to 0.75 inches, and type **Return**

If this still does not allow the figures to fit into their cells properly, then highlight the figures and change the font to a smaller size.

Draw a box around the figures from the spreadsheet by using the same technique you used to place a box around text.

4. Copying a chart from the spreadsheet

Move the cursor to the position in the document you want the chart to appear, it is suggested you place it between the text and the figures.

Pull down the **Edit** menu and select **I** (for **Insert chart**).

Select the spreadsheet name **and** the chart name you want from the dialog boxes and **Return** (make sure that both the spreadsheet name and the chart name are highlighted).

The chart does not appear but a **placeholder** (text which shows where the chart will appear when printed) will be visible in the document.

5. Looking at how the chart will actually appear

Pull down the **Print** menu and select **Preview**, you can then see how the chart will look.

6. Altering the size of the chart

It is quite possible that the chart will need to be made bigger or smaller.

After making sure that the cursor is positioned on the placeholder, pull down the **Format** menu and select **A** (for **Indents & Spacing.**)

Alter the height of the chart to 3 inches and **return**.

Print preview the file again and if it is satisfactory, print it out.

The finished result should look like this:

```
To:          Fred Jones
From:        Marketing

From:        Sally Buttons
Dept:        Sales
```

Memo

I am sending you the figures showing the profit projections for our products, these are to be distributed to the retail customers to show them how profitable it is to buy and resell these items.

I suggest you mailmerge the customers with this information.

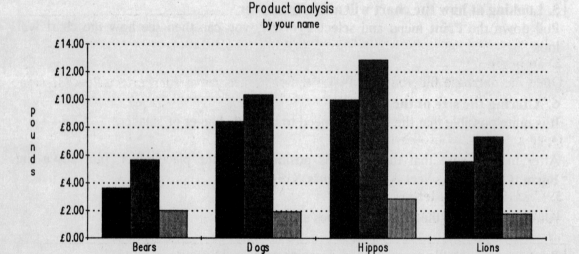

Product analysis
by your name

```
Profit Analysis by product

by your name
```

Number	Product	Cost	Sell at	Profit	Total
4	Bears	£3.65	£5.67	£2.02	£8.08
3	Dogs	£8.41	£10.35	£1.94	£5.82
6	Hippos	£9.99	£12.87	£2.88	£17.28
2	Lions	£5.55	£7.32	£1.77	£3.54
Total					£34.72

SESSION 19

Mailmerging

This section looks at mailmerging (merging a list of names and addresses from the database with a standard letter produced using the word-processing program).

---

1. Objectives
> **By the end of this session you will be able to:**
> Merge information from a database with a word processed file

---

2. To begin
Open the database file you saved with the customer names for **Perfect Pets** (session 17).

Open a **New** word-processing file.

3. Creating a form letter
Type in the following text, justify and spellcheck it.

```
Dear

I  thought  you  might  be  interested  in  seeing  the  latest  profit
forecasts  for  the  sale  of  our  cuddly  toys.  I  enclose  a  copy  of  a  memo
sent to me by the sales department.

                    Yours sincerely,



                    Fred Jones (Marketing Director)
```

Now move the cursor to the top of the letter and **Return** eight times (to create spaces).

Move the cursor back to the top of the letter, then pull down the **Edit** menu and select **F** (for **Insert Field**).

A dialog box will appear. Select the database file you are going to merge with the letter by moving the cursor and highlighting it.

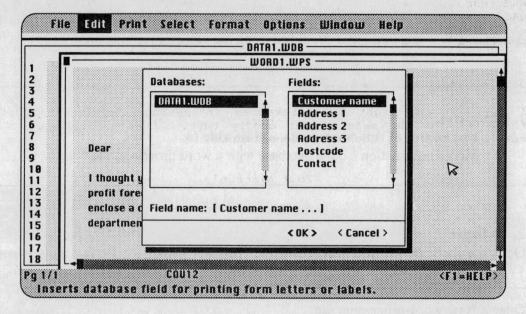

Tab to the **Fields** box and move the cursor to highlight **Customer name**, then **Return**.

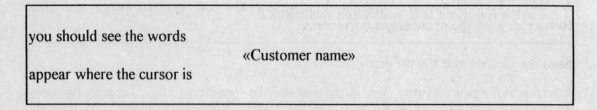

you should see the words

«Customer name»

appear where the cursor is

Move the cursor on to the next line and go through the same process, this time choosing **Address 1**.

Repeat this for **Address 2**, **Address 3** and **Postcode**.

When you have done that move the cursor one space beyond the word Dear in the first line of text (use the **spacebar**), now go through the same process (as above) for the Field **Contact**.

110

The form letter should look like this before it is merged with the datafile.

```
«Customer name »
«Address 1      »
«Address 2      »
«Address 3      »
«Postcode       »


Dear «Contact      »

I thought you might be interested in seeing the latest profit
forecasts for the sale of our cuddly toys.  I enclose a copy of a
memo sent to me by the sales department.


                    Your sincerely,



            Fred Jones (Marketing Director)
```

To print this (you cannot preview the mailmerging), pull down the **Print** menu and select **F** (for **Print Form Letters**).

A dialog box will appear, highlight the database file you want to merge and then **Return** to print the mailmerged documents.

Save the file and quit the program.

SESSION 20

Final Exercise

Objective
This is a simulation of a series of business activities where you are asked to practise the techniques you have learned. Refer to appendix 2 for help.

Scenario
You are a computer operator for a firm of sport goods wholesalers called Runners Wholesale Ltd. As part of your work you have been asked to set up the following files.

SPREADSHEET
Create a spreadsheet containing the following data:

```
Runners Wholesale Ltd

Stock Control System  - Shoes


Item Description  Ref Units In  Units Sold Balance  Cost/Unit Total Stock Sell Price  Tot Sales
Nike Air Max B1   NAMB    201       110     xxx      45.00      xxx       54.99        xxx
Nike Air Peg M    NAMP    552       445     xxx      29.56      xxx       39.99        xxx
Brooks Regent +   BRR+    132        12     xxx      39.87      xxx       59.99        xxx
Asics Gel Lyte3   AGL3    674       559     xxx      34.32      xxx       49.99        xxx
Asics 101         A101    872       212     xxx      29.43      xxx       44.99        xxx
Nike Air Terra    NATR     23         1     xxx      43.34      xxx       49.99        xxx
Nike Lady Airmax  NLAM     21        19     xxx      42.98      xxx       54.99        xxx

Totals                   xxx       xxx     xxx                 xxx                    xxx
```

```
Balance (column 5) = Units In minus Units Sold
Total Stock        = Balance times Cost/Unit
Total Sales        = Balance times Selling Price
```

Format the figures (with £ signs and two decimal places) and the text as you wish, enter formulae into the cells marked **xxx**.

Sort the product names into ascending alphabetic order.

Save your file as you will need it later on.

DATABASE
Create a database file from the following customer data:

```
Top Trainers      25 The Arcade          Chelmsford    Essex        CM11 2XE   Nike
West End Sports   75 London road         LLandudno     Gwynedd      CD23 6TF   Asics
Jogging Joyfully  The Borough            Handsworth    Birmingham   BT5 6YF    Nike
Running & Biking  110 Frederick Avenue   Southsea      Hampshire    PO8 5RE    Brooks
Image Plus        100 North End          Brighton      Sussex       BN2 7RJ    Nike
Super Sports Ltd  176 St Michaels Hill   Loughborough  Leicester    LE4 4ES    Asics
Wrights Ltd       87 Old Church Rd       Plymouth      Devon        PE1 8UH    Nike
Run Like A Fox    The Mall               Minehead      Somerset     TA4 8RE    Brooks
```

Choose field names, screen layout, formats, etc. for this datafile, trying to make them as attractive as possible. Again, save the file.

Tasks
After having set these up you are approached by the sales manager who wants you to produce a report of the customers with only their names and postcodes printed out (with suitable headings).

He also asks for a **bar chart** and an **area line graph** from the data in the following columns only:

```
Ref
Units In
Units Sold
Balance
```

To Start
Add a title and subheading to your chart and label the **X** and **Y axes** with suitable descriptions.

Alter the font for the title and the other fonts (choose the most appropriate sizes and fonts).

Send the spreadsheet figures (using the first four columns of the spreadsheet figures only) and the charts in the form of a report with your name and a message from you to the sales manager. You need to create a word-processed document and copy the figures and the chart into it.

After having looked at the data you have supplied, the sales manager decides to **mail-merge** from the datafile a letter to the customers who have only bought Asics shoes.

Hint: Use View Query

The basic (unformatted) text of the letter is as follows, please lay it out in the best way possible to get the attention of the prospective customers.

```
Customer Name and Address

Dear Customer Name,

Special Promotion

As a special pre season offer we are able to sell you Brooks and
Asics shoes at super discounts.

For example the Brooks Regents+ which retails at 89.99 and which has
a normal wholesale price of 59.99 is available at a discounted price
of 42.00.

To take advantage of these offers or to find out more, phone our
sales team on 0932-76532 (6 lines) immediately.

Yours in sport

Edgar Harris (sales manager)
```

You should end up with the following printouts:

1. Database report.
2. Word-processed report to the sales manager.
3. Mailmerged letters (2 letters in all).

APPENDICES

The appendices contain material to assist you in four ways. Firstly there is a section on how to lay out your work to best advantage, secondly a revision section dealing with the most used and useful commands you have covered. Next there is a section on how to manage your files while using Works, for example how to copy or delete files. Lastly there is a section on how to set the screen display and other settings to suit you best.

The contents are:

Appendix 1 Suggestions on layout
Appendix 2 Summary of commands
Appendix 3 File management
Appendix 4 Configuring the system

SUGGESTIONS ON LAYOUT

When laying out your work, it is worthwhile making use of the features available within a word-processing program. **WORKS** contains many sophisticated commands which can be used to enhance your work and to present it in the most favourable way.

For the purposes of this section the commands can be divided into three, **character commands**; **paragraph commands**; and **page commands**.

1. Character commands
Commands such as **bold**, *italic*, underline, can be used to make words and sentences stand out. You can also alter the size and design of the fonts (although this will to some extent depend upon the printer available).

2. Paragraph commands
Justification, double line spacing, indents, alignment (left, right or centre) are all methods of making your work look more interesting or legible. Another popular feature of **WORKS** is the **Borders** feature which enables you can draw boxes around selected text.

Please note that using the **Tab** key is a much better method of controlling spacing than using the spacebar (for hanging indents etc). While they may both look the same on the screen, when printed they may be very different.

3. Page commands
Margins, page numbering, headers and footers are some of the available features of **WORKS** which will help readers find their way around your document.

Avoid having only one or two lines of a paragraph at the top or bottom of a page as it looks ugly on the page. The **Page Break** command can be used to insert an artificial page break wherever you want it.

4. Experiment

All the above techniques should be used with restraint to avoid a chaotic looking page, but experiment with different effects to suit your purposes.

By far the most effective way of learning to lay out your work is to try different effects.

When you read books and magazines, look at the way they use fonts, margins, etc., and if you like it, try to recreate it in your work.

SUMMARY OF COMMANDS

The commands covered in this manual are as follows:

FILE COMMANDS
These are common to all **WORKS** applications:

1. Opening a file
Pull down (or click the mouse on) the **File Menu.**

Choose either to **Create a New File** or **Open** an already existing one.

2. Saving a file
Pull down the **File Menu** (if you are saving the file for the first time or wish to change its name then you should **Save As**, otherwise **Save** is quicker).

3. Previewing work before printing
Pull down the **Print Menu** and select **Preview**.

4. Printing text
Pull down the **Print Menu** and select **Print.**

5. Exiting Works
Pull down the **File Menu** and select **Exit Works**.

WORD PROCESSING

1. Character commands

Highlight the required text (either by clicking and dragging the mouse or using **F8** and the cursor keys).

bold	**Format Menu and Bold (or CTRL B)**
italic	**Format Menu and Italic (or CTRL I)**
<u>underline</u>	**Format Menu and Underline (or CTRL U)**

To remove character commands, highlight the text and **CTRL** and **Spacebar**.

To change the character fonts, highlight the text, pull down the **Format Menu** and select **Font & Style**, then highlight the fonts/size you require.

2. Paragraph commands

Centring	**Format Menu** and **Centre**
Justification	**Format Menu** and **Justified**
Double Spacing	**Format Menu** and **Double Space**
Hanging Indents	Tab the first character of the first line and then **CTRL H** (to remove hanging indents is **CTRL G**). Note that hanging indents are merely one type of indents although a widely used one.
Indents	**Format Menu** and **Indents**

To copy or move text around the document (or to another document), pull down the **Edit Menu** and select **Copy** or **Move**.

3. Setting tabs

To set tabs pull down the **Format Menu** and select **Tabs**.

4. Boxes (borders around text)

To box text, highlight the text and pull down the **Format Menu** and select Borders and then Outline and enter the type of box wanted.

To remove unwanted boxes, go to the same menu and remove any characters in the dialog boxes.

5. Page commands

To alter the margins pull down the **Print Menu** and select **Page Setup & Margins.**

To set up **Headers, Footers** and **Page Numbers**, pull down the **Print Menu** and select **Headers & Footers**.

To move quickly around the text the following keys can be used:
Ctrl Home
Ctrl End
these move to the start and end of the document.

To set page breaks where you want (to avoid lines of paragraphs appearing on different pages), move the cursor to the position you want the new page to start and press **CTRL Return**

(you should then pull down the **Options Menu** and select **Paginate Now** to reset all the other page breaks in the document).

To remove page breaks, position the cursor on the page break line (a dotted line) and delete it.

6. Spellchecking and the thesaurus

It is **always** a good idea to spellcheck your work.

To do so, pull down the **Options Menu** and select **Check Spelling.** For the Thesaurus choose **Thesaurus**.

SPREADSHEET

The Worksheet
The worksheet is where figures are entered (to switch between the worksheet and **Charting** pull down the **View** menu and select either **Spreadsheet** or the required chart you wish to display).

You can easily tell whether you are in the worksheet or the chart mode since the chart mode displays the word **CHART** along the bottom of the screen.

1. Inserting / deleting rows / columns
Pull down the **Edit** menu and select the required option.

2. Altering the width of columns
Pull down the **Format** menu and select **Column Width**.

3. Formatting cells
Highlight the cells and pull down the **Format** menu and select **Font** to alter the design or size of the characters or **Style** for bold, italic or underline.

4. Copying formulae
Highlight both the cell you wish to copy from and the cells to copy to, pull down the **Edit** menu and select **Fill right** or **Fill down.**

5. Blanking or clearing cells
Highlight the cells and pull down the **Edit** menu and select **Clear.**

6. Editing the contents of a cell
Move the cursor to the cell, press **F2** and alter the contents using the cursor keys to move along the word.

CHARTING

This is the part of the spreadsheet module where you can create charts.

1. Creating a chart

Highlight the cells to be included in the chart (normally you will want to include column headings) and pull down the **View** menu.

Select **New Chart** and a bar chart will appear.

Important: If you want to see the data shown as a different type of chart pull down the **Format** menu, select the required type of chart e.g. a line graph, and then pull down the **View** menu again and select the original chart again.

It is not necessary to create a new chart, you are merely displaying the same data in a different way.

---

2. Titles

To add titles pull down the **Data** menu and select **Titles**, enter the titles and look at the chart.

3. Altering fonts

To alter the fonts pull down the **Format** menu and select the option required.

DATABASE

This follows very similar menu structures to the word-processing and spreadsheet modules.

COPYING DATA FROM THE SPREADSHEET OR DATABASE TO A WORD PROCESSED DOCUMENT

Once you have mastered copying within an individual module, copying across modules is easy, simply follow these steps:

Make sure that all the necessary files are open.

Move the cursor to the position in the word-processed document you wish to insert the data (from the database or spreadsheet).

Move back to the spreadsheet or database file (pull down the **Window** menu and select the file).

Highlight the data required to be copied, pull down the **Edit** menu and select **Copy.**

Pull down the **Window** menu and select the word-processing file, check the cursor in still in the required position and press **return**.

You may need to tidy up the data by making the font smaller so it fits on the page (or alter the spacing).

COPYING CHARTS FROM THE SPREADSHEET TO A WORD-PROCESSED FILE

This is even easier, open both the word-processing file and the spreadsheet file.

Stay in the word-processing file and position the cursor where you want the chart to appear.

Pull down the **Edit** menu and select **Insert Chart**. Highlight the required spreadsheet file and the required chart and **return**. A placeholder appears in the document and you can see the effect by selecting **Print Preview**.

---

note
If the chart does not appear check that you have not selected **Draft** in the **Print** dialog box.

FILE MANAGEMENT

Within **Works** there are facilities for File Management which enable you to carry out necessary housekeeping activities such as deleting obsolete files. The screen is shown below:

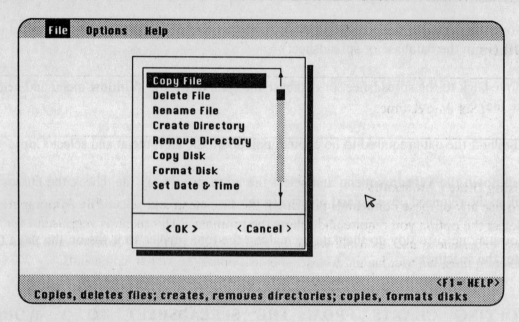

It is useful to divide these up in sections:

Disk housekeeping

Copy file
Delete file
Rename file
Copy disk
Format disk

Directory commands

> Create directory
> Remove directory

Others

> Set date & time

Using these Commands

To use any of these commands pull down the **File** menu and select **File Management**. Select the option you require and follow the prompts. This menu is very useful for the less experienced user as it allows he or she to easily carry out common activities like deleting files, without having to learn the disk operating system commands.

An example using the delete command

To get rid of surplus files it is necessary to delete them from the disk. To do this choose **Delete** from the menu and the screen will show the following:

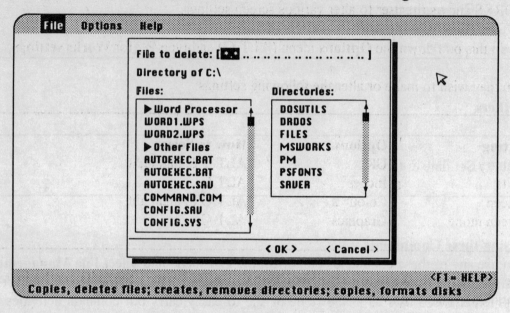

Click (or move the cursor on to) the required file name and **return**. The file will have been deleted from the disk.

Please be careful, once a file has been deleted it has gone.

CONFIGURING THE SYSTEM

WORKS allows the user to alter various screen settings.

To do this pull down the **Options** menu (**ALT O**) and type **W** (for **Works settings**).

You may wish to make or alter the following settings:

Setting	Options	How to Select
Country	UK	ALT U & highlight
Units	Inches	ALT I
Screen	Colour 2	ALT O & highlight
Screen mode	Graphics	ALT G

The various options relate to the country e.g. UK, USA etc., the units can be inches, centimetres and so on.

The screen colour is a personal choice, the graphics mode is important as although the program will run slightly slower, underlining, italics and bold etc will show on screen and you will be able to see more clearly how the finished article will look.

dBase IV for Business Students
An Active-Learning Approach

J Muir

ISBN: **1 873981 16 3** • Date: **June 1992** • Edition: **1st**
Extent: **200 pp (approx)** • Size: **245 x 190 mm**
Lecturers' Supplement ISBN: **1 873981 76 7**

This book is aimed at students on a wide variety of business courses who need to know how to use dBase IV (the industry-standard database management system for IBM PC and compatibles). The learning material in this book requires minimal, if any, input by lecturers and can be recommended for student self-instruction. It makes no assumptions about business or computing knowledge, but teaches dBase IV techniques and their business applications in simple terms.

All students can successfully use this book – from those needing only an introduction to those needing to go to advanced programming. It covers the **essentials** of dBase IV at **each** level. The text covers all three modes of dBase IV- menu-driven, command driven, and programming. dBase IV features are progressively introduced in the context of practical business activities.

Note: A copyright free $3\frac{1}{2}$" (750K) disk is provided free of charge to lecturers adopting the book as a course text. It includes all the programs, databases, etc used in the book.

Contents:

Introduction – Databases in Business • Using the Control Centre • Creating and Searching a Database • Views and Queries – Retrieving Selected Records • Modifying the Database Structure • Adding and Deleting Records • Indexing and Sorting • Producing Printed Reports • Designing Data Entry Screens • Checking User Output • The Applications Generator • Using the Dot Prompt to Create and Search a Database • Dot Prompt Commands • Creating and Running a Program • Program Debugging • Programming Using Screens, Queries and Printed Reports • Decisions and Conditions – IF and DO CASE Commands • Looping or Iteration – DO WHILE...ENDDO • Locating Duplicate Records • Using Multiple Databases – Updating and Joining • Passing Parameters Between Programs • Conclusion – Bringing It All Together.

Free Lecturers' Supplement

Oliver and Chapman's
Data Processing &
Information Technology *Revised by CS French*

"The Complete Course Text"

ISBN: **1 870941 39 X** • Date: **1990** • Edition: **8th**
Extent: **432 pp** • Size: **245 x 190 mm**
Lecturers' Supplement ISBN: **1 873981 44 9**

Courses on which this book is known to be used
ACCA; CIMA; AAT; ICSA; IComA; City and Guilds; A Level Computing; BTEC National Computer
Studies; BTEC HNC/D Business Studies; BSc Computer Studies; BSc Information Technology; IAM;
BPICS II; CIPFA; Graduate Conversion Course; HND Information and Control Systems; HNC BIT;
Combined Degree – Computing; C & G 424; BTEC National IP; BA Business Studies.

On reading lists of ACCA, AAT, IDPM, BCS, IComA, CBSI, ICM, ICSA and LCCI

This book provides a simplified approach to the understanding of data processing and information
technology. It is intended for those with little or no knowledge of the subject.

The contents have been reorganised and extensively revised to provide a modern perspective. The text
contains significant new material on work stations, structure methods, databases and 4GLs.

Contents:
Introduction to Information Systems • Computer Storage • Computer Input and Output • Computer Systems
Organisation • Computer Files • Software Development • File Processing • Software • Database Systems •
Information Systems Development • Applications • Computer Systems • Information Systems Management •
The Social Aspect • Case Exercises.

Review Comments:
'Good core text, excellent price.' *'Good value text, succinctly written.'* – **Lecturers**

*'This new edition has some very useful changes from the previous one. The wider page format helps in
presentation of the material (and reading the book). The order of the contents is more logical than the last
edition and there are some useful additions in the areas of 4GLs, databases and workstations ... The book's
strongest point is its coverage of computer technology and data processing. It has some very useful
examples throughout the text and is as up-to-date as textbooks reasonably can be.'*

"ACCA Students' Newsletter"

Also available as ELBS edition
in member countries at local
currency equivalent price
of £2.50

*Free
Lecturers' Supplement*

Management Information Systems

T Lucey

ISBN: **1 870941 80 2** • Date: **1991** • Edition: **6th**
Extent: **336 pp** • Size: **215 x 135 mm**
Lecturers' Supplement ISBN: **1 873981 59 7**

Courses on which this book is known to be used
ACCA; HND Yr 1; HNC BIS; Info. Systems Fundamentals; DAS; MSD; DBA; HNC Industrial Studies; NEBSM; CMS; IPM (PMFP); Dip. in Int. Audit; Nat. Cert. in Computer Studies; CIPFA; AAT; HND BIT; HND Computing; BSc Computing; IAM; BSc (Bus. Studies); DMS; BEd Bus. Studies; CIMA; CIML Software Eng. Man.; MSc Computing; ICSA; MBA; IMS.

On reading lists of ACCA, AAT, IComA, ABE, ICM, IAM and BCS

The book deals with the design and application of management information systems in private and public sector organisations.

For the new edition the text has been substantially updated and revised including assignments, case studies and more detail on information technology.

Contents:

Management Information Systems – An Overview • Information, Data and Communications • Systems Concepts – Structure and Elements • Systems concepts – Objectives and Types • Organisations – Principles and Structure • Organisations – Adaptability and Behaviour • Organisations – Configuration, Culture and Information Management Levels and Functions • Motivation and Leadership • Organising and Co–ordinating • Planning • Decision Making • Control – Concepts, Loops and Information • Control in Organisations • Information Technology and MIS • Influences on MIS Design • Answers to End of Chapter Questions.

Review Comments:

'...an excellent work on general management with the emphasis on MIS. I have chosen it in preference to the many management books I have recently reviewed.' 'Good coverage at an excellent price.' 'Still the best book for an introductory organisation and information systems course.' 'Easy to read and understand.' 'Excellent value as a first text on MIS.' 'Much improved edition [6th[for this syllabus [ICSA].' 'I like it for its broad management approach.' – Lecturers

'The book is highly recommended to students, to accountants and to business managers who want a simple guide to modern systems theory.'

"Management Accounting"

Also available as ELBS edition
in member countries at local
currency equivalent price
of £1.50

Spreadsheets for Business Students

An Active-Learning Approach

C West

ISBN: **1 870941 83 7** • Date: **1991** • Edition: **1st**
Extent: **176 pp** • Size: **245 x 190 mm**
Lecturers' Supplement ISBN: **1 873981 66 X**

Courses on which this book is known to be used
CBA; CMS; BA (Hons) Acc. & Fin.; BEd Bus. Studies; CLAiT II; Dip. Voc. Ed. Bus. & Fin.; HNC/D; ACCA Level 1; BA Business Studies; BTEC Nat.; HNC Bus. & Fin.; BEng; HND Computing; HND Manufacturing Management; IPM; DMS.

The aim of this book is to provide a 'user friendly' guide for students on the innumerable courses where acquaintance with the basics of spreadsheets is required.

It is very much a 'learning by doing' guide – requiring very little (if any) input by the lecturer and can be used on any machine/system with Lotus 1-2-3 version 2.0 (or above) or compatible spreadsheets such as VP-Planner and As-Easy-As.

All examples have a business emphasis and students progressively gain confidence in the basics of:

- constructing spreadsheet models
- saving and retrieving files
- graphics
- printing spreadsheets and graphs
- using a spreadsheet as a data base
- creating and using simple macros.

The lecturers' supplement is a copyright-free $5\frac{1}{4}$" (360K) PC-compatible disk, incorporating files in .WKS format for the models in the book, for checking students' activities.

Contents:

Models include:
VAT Calculations • Cash Flow Forecast • Integrated Cash Flow Forecast/ Profit & Loss Account/Balance Sheet • Accounting Ratios • Cost Behaviour • Cost Allocation and Apportionment • Cost-Volume-Profit Analysis.

Each session contains:
Objectives • Active Learning • Summary • Activities • Objective (Multi-choice) Test.

Review Comments:

'I like the worksheet approach enabling students to work at their own pace.' 'A wonderful time saver – congratulations.' 'Ideal for new modularised units – all activity based.' 'Tried it on 2 lecturers first – they found it easy, so able now to recommend it to students!' 'Good to use in open learning workshop.' 'Excellent in every way – a book like this, at its current price, has been wanted for years!' 'A very useful text – practical and easy to understand.' – Lecturers

Free
Lecturers' Supplement

Spreadsheets for Accountancy Students

An Active-Learning Approach

C West

ISBN: **1 873981 31 7** • Date: **August 1992** • Edition: **1st**
Extent: **360 pp (approx)** • Size: **245 x 190 mm**
Lecturers' Supplement ISBN: **1 873981 86 4**

Courses on which this book is expected to be used
All professional accountancy courses and accountancy degree courses, and accounting options on business courses.

The aim of the book is to provide a 'user friendly' guide for accountancy students. It is very much a 'learning by doing' guide – requiring very little (if any) input by the lecturer and can be used on any machine/system with Lotus 1-2-3 version 2.0 (or above) or compatible spreadsheets such as VP-Planner and As-Easy-As.

The book is in two parts:

Part A: Apart from minor amendments, this Part is the complete content of *Spreadsheets for Business Students* (see below) as accountancy students, starting from scratch, need a foundation of these more basic techniques before concentrating on those aspects **specific** to accountants.

Part B: This consists of a series of models, some interrelated, covering **financial accounting, management accounting,** and **financial management**. Basic skills will be learned through applying spreadsheet principles to solve accountancy problems.

The lecturers' supplement is a copyright-free PC-compatible disk, incorporating files in .WKS format for the models in the book, for checking students' activities.

Contents:

Part A – *Models include:* VAT Calculations • Cash Flow Forecast • Integrated Cash Flow Forecast/ Profit & Loss Account/Balance Sheet • Accounting Ratios • Cost Behaviour • Cost Allocation and Apportionment • Cost-Volume-Profit Analysis.

Each session contains:
Objectives • Active Learning • Summary • Activities • Objective (Multi-choice) Test.

Part B – Financial Accounting, Management Accounting and Financial Management Models

Each session contains:
Objectives • Active Learning • Problem • Model Solution: Creation and Explanation • Activity.

"The Complete Course Text"

Computer Science   *CS French*

ISBN: **1 873981 19 8** • Date: **June 1992** • Edition: **4th**
Extent: **450 pp (approx)** • Size: **275 x 215 mm**
Lecturers' Supplement ISBN: **1 873981 41 4**

Courses on which this book is known to be used
A Level Computing; BTEC National and HNC/D Computer Studies; City & Guilds; BCS; AS Level
Computer Science; BSc Applied Science.
On reading lists of ICM, IDPM, BCS and ACP

This book provides a simplified approach to the understanding of Computer Science.

Notes on the Fourth Edition

This edition contains changes in content and layout which are aimed not just at covering the material on the
latest syllabuses but at assisting the reader's study **for the latest examinations**. Parts targeted at
contemporary computer applications and applications packages have been introduced. This reflects a
significant shift in emphasis in examinations over recent years. Graphical User Interfaces (GUIs),
development methodologies, desktop computers, applications packages and databases have been given
more emphasis to reflect the examination requirements of developing and using computer systems.
Obsolete material has been removed.

Contents:

Foundation Topics • Applications I: Document Processing • Storage • Input and Output • Applications II:
GUIs and Multimedia • Computer Systems Organisation I • Programming I • File and File Processing •
Applications III: Spreadsheets • Logic and Formal Notations • Computer Arithmetic • Computer Systems
Organisation II • Software • Applications IV: Applications Areas • Programming II • Databases and 4GLs •
Applications V: Information Storage and Retrieval • Systems Development • Applications VI: Business
Industrial Computing • Computers in Contexts • Revision Test Questions.

Review Comments:

*'I think the presentation is superb and content perfect for my course work.' 'Good basic book –
recommended by all academic staff in the department.' – **Lecturers***

Free Lecturers' Supplement

Computing
An Active-Learning Approach

PM Heathcote

ISBN: **1 870941 86 1** • Date: **1991** • Edition: **1st**
Extent: **352 pp** • Size: **275 x 215 mm**
Lecturers' Supplement ISBN: 1 873981 37 6

> *Courses on which this book is known to be used*
> A Level Computing; BTEC Nat and Higher; ACCA Info Systems; BSc Software Eng; C & G 419 (DP);
> BTEC Cont Ed; BTEC First; Access to Computing; BTEC Nat Eng; AS;
> C & G 726; BA Business Studies.

The aim of this book is to provide the classroom support material needed on Advanced Level Computing and BTEC courses.

There are many excellent textbooks on computing at this level (including *Computer Science* by CS French) which give valuable support and wider reading/reference for the student outside classroom time.

This book, however, has been designed as an interactive teaching and learning aid, eliminating the need for hand outs or copious note taking. It incorporates the following features:

- concise explanation of principles

- questions at appropriate points within the text (with space allowed for student to fill in answers) to enable the student to test and broaden knowledge and understanding, develop ideas, supply discussion points and test application of principles.

Teachers can explain each part of a topic in whatever way they like and use the concise explanations as the 'skeleton' of the classroom work. Students take an active part in the learning process via the questions interspersed throughout the text.

Apart from its value during the course, this is also an ideal book around which each student can build his/her revision programme.

The lecturers' supplement is in the form of a PC-compatible disk. It provides tips on implementation of the course and outline answers to all in-text questions and chapter-end exercises and examination questions.

Contents:
Introduction to Computers and Business Data Processing • Programming in Pascal • Data Structures • Databases • Systems Development • Programming Languages, Compilers and Interpreters • Internal Organisation of Computers • Operating Systems and Networks • Peripherals • Computer Applications and Social Implications.

Review Comments:
'Excellent for encouraging student participation.' 'Can be used as a course companion for all Computing modules (BTEC).' 'Excellent presentation – in line with both our syllabus and teaching methods.' 'Brilliant! A very comprehensive text – really welcome [BTEC HNC Computer Studies].' 'Excellent for open learning students.' 'Brilliant book – excellent learning approach.' 'Clear, explicit, novel approach.' – Lecturers

Free
Lecturers' Supplement